FATAL DISTRACTIONS

87 of the Very Best Ways to Get Beaten, Eaten, Maimed, and Mauled on Your PC

DAVID GERROLD

special game consulting
by Dennis Gerrold

WAITE GROUP PRESS™
Corte Madera, California

Publisher: *Mitchell Waite*
Editor-in-Chief: *Scott Calamar*
Editorial Director: *Joel Fugazzotto*
Managing Editor: *John Crudo*
Assistant Editor: *Joanne Miller*
Content Editor: *Heidi Brumbaugh*
Copy Editor: *Kathy Carlyle*
Technical Reviewer: *Scott Rhoades*
Production Director: *Julianne Ososke*
Design and Production: *Karen Johnston*
Illustrations: *Laura Nichols*
Cover Design: *Rogondino & Associates*
Cover Illustration: *Will Cormier*

Published by Waite Group Press™, 200 Tamal Plaza, Corte Madera, CA 94925.
Waite Group Press is distributed to bookstores and book wholesalers by Publishers Group West, Box 8843, Emeryville, CA 94662, 1-800-788-3123 (in California 1-510-658-3453).

Printed in the United States of America
94 95 96 97 • 10 9 8 7 6 5 4 3 2 1

Gerrold, David, 1944-
Fatal distractions: 87 of the very best ways to get beaten, eaten, maimed, and mauled on your PC / David Gerrold; special game consulting by Dennis Gerrold.
p. cm.
Includes index.
ISBN: 1-878739-77-8: $26.95 ($37.95 Can.)
1. Computer games. 2. Computer games -- Software. I. Title.
GV1469.15.G47 1994 94-21595
794.8--dc20 CIP

DEDICATION

for Jeff and Carol Duntemann, with love

THANK YOU!

Graeme Cree
James P. Fisher III
Carlton Griffin
Tom Hall
Hank Leukart
Dean Luick
Dave & Ann Malmberg
Randall Penn
Mark Rein
Joe Siegler
Stanley Stasiak
Doug Steele
Mike Stephenson
Janet Walz
Jay Wilbur
Paul Winner
and many others

TABLE OF CONTENTS

CONTENTS

Contents

Contents

WAITE
GROUP
PRESS™

Dear Reader:

What is a book? Is it perpetually fated to be inky words on a paper page? Or can a book simply be something that inspires—feeding your head with ideas and creativity regardless of the medium? The latter, I believe. That's why I'm always pushing our books to a higher plane; using new technology to reinvent the medium.

I wrote my first book in 1973, *Projects in Sights, Sounds, and Sensations*. I like to think of it as our first multimedia book. In the years since then, I've learned that people want to *experience* information, not just passively absorb it—they want interactive MTV in a book. With this in mind, I started my own publishing company and published *Master C,* a book/disk package that turned the PC into a C language instructor. Then we branched out to computer graphics with *Fractal Creations,* which included a color poster, 3-D glasses, and a totally rad fractal generator. Ever since, we've included disks and other goodies with most of our books. *Virtual Reality Creations* is bundled with 3-D Fresnel viewing goggles and *Walkthroughs & Flybys CD* comes with a multimedia CD-ROM. We've made complex multimedia accessible for any PC user with *Ray Tracing Creations, Multimedia Creations, Making Movies on your PC, Image Lab,* and three books on Fractals.

The Waite Group continues to publish innovative multimedia books on cutting-edge topics, and of course the programming books that make up our heritage. Being a programmer myself, I appreciate clear guidance through a tricky OS, so our books come bundled with disks and CDs loaded with code, utilities, and custom controls.

By 1995, The Waite Group will have published 150 books. Our next step is to develop a new type of book, an interactive, multimedia experience involving the reader on many levels. With this new book, you'll be trained by a computer-based instructor with infinite patience, run a simulation to visualize the topic, play a game that shows you different aspects of the subject, interact with others on-line, and have instant access a large database on the subject. For traditionalists, there will be a full-color, paper-based book.

In the meantime, they've wired the White House for hi-tech; the information super highway has been proposed; and computers, communication, entertainment, and information are becoming inseparable. To travel in this Digital Age you'll need guidebooks. The Waite Group offers such guidance for the most important software—your mind.

We hope you enjoy this book. For a color catalog, just fill out and send in the Reader Report Card at the back of the book.

Sincerely,

Mitchell Waite

Mitchell Waite
Publisher

"FORWARD"

Want to have some fun? Of course, you do. That's why you bought your computer. The computer is the very best toy ever invented. It expands our ability to play. It lets us travel in realms of wonder where the rules of reality are whatever we want them to be. There are no limits in cyberspace. If it can be dreamed, it can be evoked. Welcome to the domains of imagination. No king, no emperor, ever had the marvelous toys that we take for granted.

It's been a long time coming.

In February of 1973, I was in the city of Boston, attending Boskone, one of the nation's more intelligent annual science fiction conventions. I had just published a novel called *When Harlie Was One,* about the world's first self-aware intelligence engine. The book had received some surprisingly nice reviews, as well as a Hugo and Nebula nomination. (I will not so humbly point out that it was also the first science fiction novel ever to use a computer virus as a plot point.) It also brought me lots of friendly letters from computer students and other techno-compulsives; I received invitations to a lot of remarkable places I never would have seen otherwise – including M.I.T.'s computer labs.

I remember two things about that 1973 visit. The first was an astonishing electric train layout that stretched across two or three or four classrooms. I never did get to see it all, and because it was late in the evening, nothing was running. I have no idea *why* the Massachusetts Institute of Technology would want to have several of its classrooms permanently filled with several hundred scale miles of model railroad track, trains, and scenery, but I suspect that underneath all of the other explanations, there was a healthy recognition that at the heart of learning is *playing.*

What I saw next, however, almost had me going back to school as a computer major. My hosts walked me into a laboratory filled with arcane-looking electronics. Tall towering units with flashing lights on their front panels. Naked keyboards with no typewriters attached. Humongous monochrome monitors, some of them only naked cathode ray tubes on a chassis, others sitting in dark metal cases. Wires everywhere. All that was missing was an elevator table with a shrouded body and two kites to catch the lightning from the clouds. It was heaven.

Now, remember, this was 1973. At that time, *all* computers were believed to be room-filling monsters; even the smallest was the size of a couple refrigerators, and packed with enough colored wire to decorate the Rockefeller Center Christmas Tree. They were kept in air-conditioned vaults because they wouldn't run if they overheated. The machines were tended by a special priesthood and mere mortals were not allowed into the sacred presence.

There were no video games yet – even Pong had not yet been invented, let alone Pac Man – and the Bowmar Brain, a four-function calculator, still cost over a hundred dollars. The first Altair wouldn't be shown in the pages of *Popular Science* for another couple of years. Nobody drooled at the name Imsai, let alone TRS-80. Jobs and

Wozniak were in high school. And Bill Gates hadn't yet written his first version of BASIC.

Understand this. Before those first exciting days that most people now recall as "the computer revolution," there was an earlier revolution – the revolution that made the computer revolution not only possible, but inevitable: it was the breakthrough in vision. Suddenly there was a new kind of computer user; he didn't carry around packs of punch cards; he accessed the computer with a keyboard and a screen. That might not seem like such a major difference, but it was, because suddenly the relationship between machine and user had become one of instantaneous response. Suddenly it was *possible* for a user to think of himself as truly *interacting* with the computer.

In those days, a "hacker" wasn't a criminal, he was a code-cowboy. He was a pioneer. Every piece of code was an adventure. Nobody was a millionaire yet, nobody even had a lawyer. There was a wild spirit of cooperation, discovery, and experimentation. And this is where the *real* computer revolution happened, at least a decade before the rest of us knew about it.

Because it was here that the computer was first turned into a toy.

That's pretty profound, when you think about it. It reveals who we really are as a species. We love to play. We build multimillion dollar machines to amplify the power of our brains, to handle millions of bits of information, to make our society run smoother, and what's one of the first things we do with them? We turn them into supertoys.

Well, yes. Because the heart of learning is playing.

THE FIRST ADVENTURE

My hosts sat me down at one terminal after another to show me all the different ways they had turned the M.I.T. computers into an electronic playground. The machines themselves weren't here, they were all on the floor below; the terminals were the access.

First, I was shown the original Colossal Cave Adventure by Will Crowther and Don Woods. If you've seen it, you know how addicting it is. If you've been around longer than last Tuesday, you know that the game is the first real computer classic.

When you first sit down to play Adventure, the game seems simple enough. It's all done with text – and your imagination. You're in a magical cave, and there are many wonderful treasures here for the taking, but there are also angry little dwarves who will kill you for trespassing. There are other dangers too, including a fire-breathing dragon, a ferocious bear, and a pirate who will steal your treasure.

The terminal (or the teletype) prints a description of your location. It tells you where you are and what objects are present, you type in simple instructions like "take food," "go south," "light lamp," and "kill dwarf." Then the game reports what happens in response or where you're moved to, and you give it another command. The descriptions of the cave are fairly simple – "you are in a magnificent chamber" – but they are sufficient to trigger powerful images in your mind.

Yes, there were computer games prior to Adventure, but most of them were simple things like Hunt-The-Wumpus and Tic-Tac-Toe. They were demonstrations much more than games. You played them only for a few moments to see how they worked, you did not seek them out as recreation. So Adventure was a very important breakthrough. The cave was filled with interesting puzzles and an impish sense of humor. The deeper you explored the environment, the *more* it exercised your imagination – the more real it became. The feedback was immediate and often surprising. The wit and personalities of the authors were clearly evident.

It only takes about five minutes for a person to become hooked on Adventure. It takes at least two intense weeks of dedicated exploring and mapping to solve all the puzzles in the colossal cave, often longer. There's a lot of cave to explore. Coming back to Earth is a visceral shock.

I could have happily played Adventure for the next few hours, and later on, I was given ample opportunity to do so. I played until 3:00 in the morning. They finally had to drag me away from the terminal. This might be odd for a novelist to say, but few novels had ever hooked me the way Adventure did. What a marvelous sense of exploration and discovery it evoked. It was a tantalizing glimpse into a whole new realm of literature. Even today, Adventure is still elegant, but in 1973, it was nothing less than mind-boggling. I kept saying, "I want this, I want this. How soon can I have one of these at home?" And the fellows in the M.I.T. computer lab kept laughing and saying, "You can have one right now. All you need is fifty thousand dollars." Obviously, I wasn't the first one to ask.

SPACE WAR

The next thing I was shown was Space War.

There was a huge black-and-white cathode ray tube – just the tube in a black chassis, no case – and the screen was large and round. A single keyboard sat in front of it. One player used the keys on the left side of the keyboard, the other player used the keys on the right. Each player controlled the movements of a tiny spaceship.

In this microcosm, Newton's laws of motion ruled. Objects in motion stayed in motion. Objects at rest rested. To change either of those states, you had to fire a rocket in the opposite direction of the force you wanted to apply. It was a true hands-on experience of a deep-space environment. And to make it all even more interesting, there was a nice dense star in the center of the screen – a large gravitational mass that would pull your ship off course if you came too close, sometimes whipping it right back the way you came. Then, after you mastered the trick of navigating in a frictionless environment, you had to learn how to control your missiles and your beams and your shields.

Then you were ready for combat against an opponent.

You had one side of the keyboard, he had the other. Although the hand action did get a little crowded sometimes, Space War was the first true video game. More than that, it was the first arcade combat game where two players bashed away at each other – and it all happened in *real time*.

That was the most amazing thing. You could actually fly your own spaceship! You could put it in orbit around the star and play with trajectories, vectors, and orbital mechanics. You could begin to understand that dogfights in space are definitely *not* going to be like dogfights in an atmosphere. I finally turned to my hosts and asked, "I don't suppose this one is going to be any cheaper than the other one?" They just laughed and told me I hadn't seen anything yet.

NETWORK MAZE

Next came the biggest mind-boggler of all. I may be misremembering, but I think it was simply called The Maze.

My hosts took me to a cubbyhole and sat me down at a terminal and a keyboard. On the terminal was a very simple graphic of the interior view of a maze. It was all white lines on a black screen. There were three other users in the maze, connected by network. If you found them, you could shoot them. If they found you, they could shoot you....

I explored the maze for a little bit, found a cubbyhole where I could keep my back to the wall, and whenever someone passed by, I shot them. This did not win me any friends, but it kept me from getting killed. It was the trap-door spider technique. As much fun as Adventure and Space War were, Network Maze was the most invigorating of all the games, simply because of the knowledge that I was playing against human – and very unpredictable – opponents.

FATAL DISTRACTIONS

All three of these games had one very interesting thing in common. You could get killed real easy. These were the first "fatal distractions." I think that's the common denominator of the most interesting computer games – that there's something at stake. You can *lose*.

In real life, what qualifies an experience as an adventure is that it has an element of risk. In a computer adventure, risk is balanced against gain. Explorers in the Colossal Cave try to gather treasures and not get caught by the pirate. Pac Man gobbles through the maze trying to eat the cherries while eluding the ghosts. In Wolfenstein 3D, the Nazis chase you through their castle while you recover their stolen treasures. The very best computer games have balanced the risks against the prizes so that the challenge is just difficult enough to be interesting, but not so daunting as to be impossible.

And that brings me to the concept of *playability*.

In preparing this book and CD-ROM, we looked at hundreds of shareware games, sometimes as many as twenty or thirty a day. We rejected many more than we kept. Some were easy to eliminate from consideration. They weren't playable. Or worse, they weren't fun. Very quickly, we began to get a very good sense of what distinguishes a great computer game.

There has to be enough challenge to be interesting, but not so much difficulty as to be impossible. Here are the seven basic elements of playability:

Interface: The game screen should be attractive and interesting to look at. The game sounds should provide consistent audio cues to the player's circumstances. Overall, the interface should encourage interaction.

Feedback: The game should provide immediate response to the user's actions. The responses should be of an appropriate scale to the action.

Environment: The circumstances of the game should be easily understandable. The player must experience control over his role in the situation.

Balance: The game should have the right balance of gain and risk, effort and reward, action and reaction. The player should never feel as though the game has unfairly trapped him without also providing a means of escape.

Solvability: The problem should have enough difficulty to be challenging, but it should not be impossible. The player's actions must provide perceptible progress toward resolution.

Surprises: Along the way, there should be unexpected setbacks and reverses to complicate the problem. Equally, there should be unexpected bonuses and surprises, but only where appropriate.

Depth: The game should reveal new levels of itself as the player proceeds. The action must not be repetitious. Like a great novel, a great game should have an intriguing beginning, a fascinating development, and an astonishing resolution.

What we're really talking about here are ways of lowering the *frustration factor*. The player wants to *play* the game. Anything that stops that participation, anything that interrupts the flow of game action increases the frustration factor.

For instance, in some scrolling-action games, it's very easy to get killed. When you get killed, you're sent back to the very beginning, so much of your game play involves retracing the same steps over and over. This can be *very* frustrating. At the point at which the frustration outweighs the enjoyment, the player discards the game in disgust.

Regretfully, we had to discard several games that were beautifully implemented, that looked as though they would be great fun, and that we initially thought would be certain for inclusion in this collection. Why? Because the frustration factor was too high. We never did experience a feeling of *playability*.

The games in this collection were selected more for their ability to entertain than for their ability to impress.

BACK TO THE FUTURE

I want to mention two other computer programs that I saw demonstrated at M.I.T. in 1973.

The first was a simple speech synthesis program. If you typed in a phonetic sentence, the program would speak – albeit very mechanically – the phrase back to you. Laboriously, I typed in the phonetics for the phrase, "It's time to get science fiction out of the classroom and back into the gutter where it belongs," and a true science-fictional device, a talking computer, agreed with me.

The second program was one of the very first implementations of ELIZA, a synthetic conversationalist. It's amazing how much a machine can simulate interest simply by saying, "Tell me more about that," or "How does that make you feel?" Some very real-sounding conversations were possible with ELIZA.

I mention these because synthesized sound has become an essential part of many computer games, and synthesized personalities are becoming a very important part of the most sophisticated role-playing and exploration games. In 1973, all of the foundations had already been laid: Adventure was the first virtual exploration game, Space War was the first real-time action game, and Network Maze brought multiple players into the same virtual reality. All that remained was to put a machine on the desktop that was both powerful and affordable.

A few months later, I had dinner with a local computer scientist. When I mentioned what I'd seen at M.I.T., he dismissed the games as mere toys. What he said next has stuck with me for more than twenty years. He said that there were only six types of computer games: shoot-em-ups, mazes, kingdom management, strategy games, simulations, and puzzles. (I think those were the categories.) Everything else was a variation.

From a philosophical standpoint, he may have been right, but the ingenuity of thousands of programmers has clearly demonstrated how wrong he *really* was. The evidence fills our table of contents. A quick glance will show you just how many different kinds of games those first six types have evolved to become.

We've tried to organize this collection into essential categories, based on their overall similarities, but many shareware games defy easy categorization, or are so unique that they are a category unto themselves.

Take a look at the typical Apogee scrolling-action game, Crystal Caves, for example – is it a variation on Pac Man? You try to capture energy packs while not being eaten by monsters. Or is it a different kind of Adventure? You have a vast environment to explore, filled with treasures and demons. Or is it a puzzle-solving game? You have to find the right key to open the right door. If the game is played in real time, does that make it the same as Space War? Some of the games in this collection can be played on a network against other players, just like Network Maze.

In fact, *most* of these games have mixed elements of the six basic game types, so the easy classifications no longer hold true.

THE BEST GAMES OF ALL

What is true is that our games have become wonderful places to reinvent ourselves. We can become heroes and heroines of all flavors.

The first game of Adventure has spawned a thousand and more ways to play. It was the excitement of finding out just how many different ways there are to play that lured me into doing this book in the first place. Our singular goal was to find *the very best shareware games available for the PC.*

The search took Mitch Waite (the publisher), John Crudo (the editor), and me to swap meets, on-line bulletin boards, CompuServe, mail order shareware catalogs, and even the local bookstores. We prowled through bins of floppy disks and searched through more than thirty CD-ROM collections. To duplicate our search, you would have to spend literally *thousands* of dollars and at least a year of dedicated game-playing to the exclusion of all other concerns.

"Forward"

Our goal was not to assemble the *most* games, but the *best* games – the ones that you really spend time playing.

We think we've succeeded far beyond our original expectations. We're sure that you'll find this collection to be one of the most remarkable shareware collections you've ever purchased. This is the "desert island" disc. If you're only going to take one CD-ROM with you, this is the one. You could spend the rest of your life with these games and never have a boring day.

The book is *loosely* organized as a history of computer games. The first few chapters acknowledge the classic ancestors of today's top hits. You'll find text adventure games, including Colossal Cave and Dungeon, the predecessor of Zork. We've even included the Adventure Game Toolkit so you can write your own. You'll find text-graphic adventures too, classics like Castle and Hack, and the latest version of Nethack.

From there, we move into re-creations of arcade classics, puzzles, board games, and Tetris-like challenges. You'll find some wonderful surprises in this section. Hexxagon will keep you up late into the night. Nyet 3: Revenge of the Mutant Stones will have you laughing out loud. Chinese Checkers will reawaken your love of this fabulous childhood classic. Then we'll look at shoot-em-ups and combat games. It's a long way from Space Invaders to Zone 66! And you're going to be astonished by Raptor!

And then . . . in the *second half* of the book, we'll show you what amazing programs the simple adventure game has evolved into. You may have seen Duke Nukem and Jill of the Jungle, but wait till you see Halloween Harry, Xargon, and God of Thunder!

And finally, we'll take you into the astonishing world of 3D adventures. These are the games that give you a point-of-view window into a whole new world. Wolfenstein 3D is the most famous of all 3D games, and we've devoted a whole section to it. We've also included Apogee's latest big hit, Blake Stone!

And then . . . there's Doom.

You have never seen anything like Doom. If you play only one game in this collection, play Doom. You will never be the same. (You may not thank us for it, though. For sheer terror, Doom more than lives up to its name.)

Whatever kind of game you like, you're going to find it well represented in this collection. You'll probably find some old friends here. Some of these games have been widely circulated, and their fame is well-earned. Others are unknown treasures, not as commonly distributed. We're certain, however, that you're going to find many hours of delightful adventure in this collection.

We've also set aside chapters to acknowledge publishers of extraordinary merit. Apogee, ID, and Epic MegaGames have advanced the state of the art in shareware games to the point that many commercial products have been put to shame by comparison. Each of these publishers has established its own unique style of gaming, and each has been responsible for some of the very best games available anywhere. We've collected the most outstanding games from each of these publishers and put them into their own special sections. You'll see for yourself who is pushing the leading edge of game design.

Whatever your interest, we're sure that you're going to have many extraordinary hours of entertainment with the games on this CD-ROM. We know we did!

GAMES OF SPECIAL MERIT

All of the games in this collection were chosen because they are the best in their categories. They have set the standard of excellence for the entire industry. But even among the best, some efforts are so remarkable that they deserve special attention. We have highlighted these games with the trophy icon. These are the games that we felt were *outstanding* and *exceptional.*

These masterpieces are the products of extraordinary programming efforts by their authors. They are distinguished by their playability, by their wit and grace, and by their ability to provide unending astonishment, delight, and enjoyment. These are the best of the best.

The trophy will steer you right to these games. Many of them are already classics. They have carved out their own special niche in history and redefined the way all of us play with our computers. Make no mistake, these are the Hall of Famers!

SUITABLE FOR CHILDREN

Throughout this book, you will find specific games highlighted with a smiling computer. These games are especially suitable for the younger game players in your family.

Several of the games in this book are specifically *not* suitable for impressionable children because of their violent content. Suitable advisories are made in the text.

As always, it is up to the parent to assume the final responsibility for what games are allowed on the computer.

SHAREWARE

Some of the games in this collection are in the public domain. They may be freely copied and distributed, without restriction.

Other games here are freeware. The authors continue to hold the copyrights on the games, but generously allow their work to be copied and distributed.

But *most* of the games here are *shareware*. The distinction is an important one. Shareware is try-before-you-buy software. The games are copyrighted to the authors. With certain restrictions, usually acknowledged in the license.doc file, shareware games may be copied and distributed on floppy disks, bulletin boards, CD-ROMs, or through legitimate shareware distributors.

But – your copy of the program is for *limited* use only. Consider it a *free* trial. If you like the program, if you continue to use it, you are expected to pay for it. You pay for it by sending a registration fee to the author.

All of us at The Waite Group strongly encourage you to pay the registration fees for the games you like most in this collection. Many shareware authors depend on registration fees for a large part of their income. Your support is truly appreciated. And every registration counts.

The Benefits of Registering

When you support a shareware author, you are paying him for his time and effort. You are enabling him to provide technical support to users who need it, and you are giving him the resources to add important new features to his product. Most importantly, you will become eligible for expanded versions of the software, and you will receive information on upgrades and other products by the same company.

Some authors release their games as trilogies. The first episode is freely distributed, and when you register, you receive the next two episodes in the game. Some authors make hint books and cheat codes available only to registered users. And some authors provide additional parts for the game when you pay your registration fee.

Whatever the incentive, registering your favorite shareware is a great way to say thanks to the men and women who have worked so hard to entertain you. When you consider the cost of the game against how many hours of enjoyment it provides, you'll find that most shareware games have a per-hour cost far less than the price of a movie or a paperback book – and there are few books or movies that can give you the same adrenaline rush of victory.

So, please, register your shareware.

And when you do, tell them that you found their game in David Gerrold's collection of *Fatal Distractions.*

THE NEXT ADVENTURE?

Even as we go to press, we are already hearing from some of our very favorite authors about the great games they are preparing for the future. You can count on there being a follow-up edition. As long as the gamers keep inventing wonderful new ways to be beaten, eaten, maimed, and mauled, we're committed to keeping this collection current.

If you are a game author and you have a game that you think should be included, please send us a copy. We'd love to see anything new and unusual.

If you are a game player and you have found some wonderful treasure that you think we have overlooked, please send us a copy. We'll get in touch with the author and seek out the appropriate permissions.

Write to: Fatal Distractions
c/o Waite Group Press
200 Tamal Plaza, Suite 101
Corte Madera, CA 94925

Thanks!

BEFORE YOU GET YOURSELF KILLED...

You're probably eager to leap into Fatal Distractions. But before you get eaten, beaten, maimed, and mauled, you'll need to know how to use the CD. Please take a moment to read this information before you attempt to run the CD.

REQUIREMENTS

Before you can play *all* of the games included on the CD, your PC should have:

- a 386 CPU or better
- 4MB RAM or better
- a CD-ROM drive
- a hard disk drive

In addition, many of the games support:

- A mouse and/or joystick
- Sound Blaster-compatible sound boards

THE INSTALLATION PROGRAM

> Many computer games include data files that keep track of things like high scores or player statistics; these files are frequently rewritten during the course of play. Since CDs are designed only to be read from (and not written to), you may encounter problems if you attempt to play the games directly from the CD.

The Fatal Distractions CD includes an installation program that copies games of your choice from the CD to your hard disk. You can select any combination of games, as long as there is enough space available on your hard drive. (The program lets you know.)

To start the installation program, boot up your PC, place the Fatal Distractions CD in your CD-ROM drive, then type:

[CD Drive]: (ENTER)

Instead of *[CD Drive]*:, type the letter for your CD drive—**d:**, **e:**, etc. Then type:

cd (ENTER)
fatal (ENTER)

After a moment, the main screen (see Figure 1-1) appears. The games are organized on the CD just as they are in the book, so if you like a game described in Chapter 12 of the book, you'll find it on the CD in the section "Chapter 12: Apogee Software."

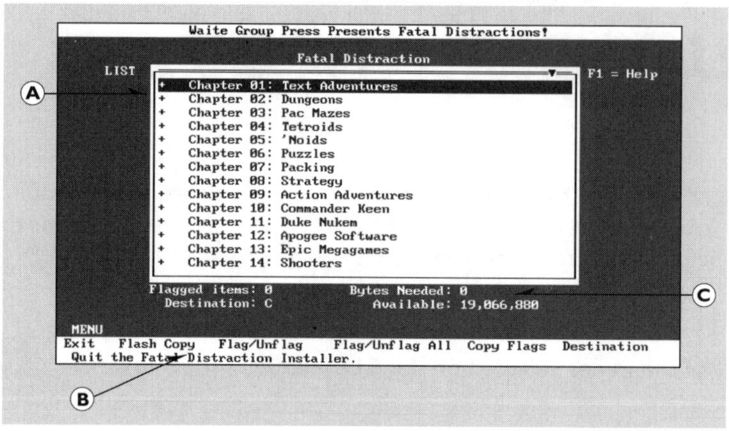

Figure I-1 This is the main screen. To locate a game from Chapter 12 of *Fatal Distractions*, highlight "Chapter 12: Apogee Software," then press ENTER.

The main features of the Installation Program are:

A) List allows you to select games or groups of games for copying; use the ↑ or ↓ to highlight different items. Move to the menu by pressing TAB.

B) Menu determines what action to take for selected games or groups of games; use the ← and → to highlight different options. Move the list by pressing TAB.

C) System Display shows how many items are selected for copying, where they're going to be copied to, how much disk space they require, and how much is available on the destination drive.

Selecting and Copying Games

To copy a game to your hard disk, follow these steps:

1. Move the highlight bar to the List by pressing TAB.
2. Locate the game(s) you want to copy. Highlight the appropriate chapter, then press ENTER to see its contents in the List.
3. Highlight the game of choice and press F to flag it for copying. You can flag as many different games as you want; pressing A flags *all* items in the list.
4. The Installation Program will normally create a directory on the C: drive called FATAL, and each game gets copied into its own subdirectory there. If you prefer a different destination, press D, then enter the drive and directory you prefer.
5. To begin copying the selected games, press C. The program creates a directory on the destination drive called FATAL, and each game gets copied into its own subdirectory there.

And remember that you can get help by pressing F1.

Flash Copying

If you are eager to play a certain game, you can Flash Copy it to your hard disk. As long as no games have been flagged for copying, the Flash Copy option is available to you. To Flash Copy a game, simply highlight the desired game, then press (C).

Status Symbols

In addition to the System Display, and help screens, three small icons appear in the List to provide additional information. These symbols (see Figure I-2) may appear at the left of items in the List:

+ - indicates that there is additional material within this item

► - indicates the complete item, including all items within it, has been flagged for copying

◄ - indicates that some items within this one have been flagged for copying

Now What? (Playing the Games)

After you've finished copying games to the hard disk, return to the DOS prompt by pressing (X), then (Y). The program returns you to the hard disk directory of the last game you copied. If you didn't copy any games, you'll return to the FATAL directory on the CD.

The game writeups in *Fatal Distractions* include a profile summarizing each game's registration info, directory name on the hard disk (unless you specified a different destination when copying) and CD, archive file, and—perhaps most importantly—what to type to play the game.

To play a game, make sure you are in the proper directory on the hard drive. Type the command listed in the profile (next to "To Play"), then press (ENTER).

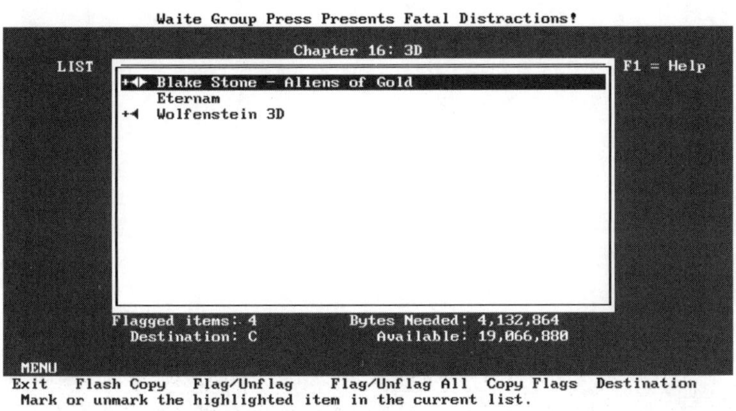

Figure I-2: The display indicates both Blake Stone - Aliens of Gold and Wolfenstein 3D have items flagged for copying, but only Blake Stone is flagged for complete copying.

MEMORY PROBLEMS

Some of these games require a good portion of free system memory before they can be played. If you are having difficulty loading or running a game, try making a clean boot disk or (if your system has DOS 6.x) try running DOS Memmaker. Refer to your DOS manual for information on either of these procedures.

Memory Management in a Multimedia World, by Joel Powell, offers advice and solutions that can help solve such memory problems. You can find it at your local book store or order it directly from Waite Group Press (there's an order form at the back of this book.)

ARCHIVES

Every game on the CD has a corresponding archive identified in the game profiles in the book. The archives compress all the game files into a single, much smaller file. The archives are saved on the CD in a directory called ARCHIVES. You won't need the archives to run the games, since the Installation Program copies the ready-to-run game to your hard disk. However, the archives provide a way for you to share these games with friends. You can copy the files to disk using the DOS Copy command; your DOS manual will explain how. (The "zipped" archives must be decompressed using the program PKUNZIP; you can obtain PKUNZIP from the shareware sources listed in this book.)

CHAPTER 1

TEXT ADVENTURES

TEXT ADVENTURES

You sit at the computer. You type simple, two-word commands. The computer responds with short paragraphs of description. There are no pictures. Everything is done in text.

Compared to today's virtual reality spectaculars, this doesn't sound very impressive, does it? But before the widespread availability of VGA-quality graphics, text mode was the only way to have a computer adventure.

Nevertheless, it worked. Text-mode adventures were the most popular category of computer game for many years. Why? Because the graphics of your own imagination are always spectacular.

Even today, the classic text adventures still retain their power to evoke the most marvelous images.

THE COLOSSAL CAVE

```
Somewhere nearby is Colossal Cave, where others have found fortunes in treasure and gold, though it
is rumored that some who enter are never seen again. The object of the game is for you to explore
the cave and return (safely) with as much treasure as possible. The cave is a mysterious and magical
place. You will face many puzzling and perilous challenges as you explore.
```

The very *first* adventure game was written sometime in the very early seventies, by Will Crowther, a researcher at Bolt, Beranek, and Newman, the Cambridge, Massachusetts research firm which built the ARPAnet, one of the first nationwide computer networks.

One of Crowther's hobbies was cave-exploration – spelunking. Occasionally, he would drive down to Kentucky to join other spelunkers in exploring Bedquilt Cave, a huge cavern connected to Mammoth Cave. Because Crowther stored topographic data of the caves in BBN's computers for the production of maps, the first Adventure program was mostly a simulated exploration of a real cave.

Don Woods, a computer student at Stanford found this first Adventure in the Xerox research computer and expanded it into a complete game. Woods added most of the features of the version called Original Adventure, but the descriptions and geology, of the first few levels of the game at least, remain analogous to actual rooms and features of the Bedquilt Cave in Kentucky.

Written in FORTRAN, the game was played on PDP-10 and DEC-20 computers. It spread rapidly across the ARPAnet. (It has since become the Internet.) At that time, the ARPAnet connected computer science departments and other research institutions all over the country. Adventure spread through all of them, quickly becoming one of the largest productivity destroyers in the nation.

The game also spread to the corporate world – wherever mainframes were installed. Everywhere Adventure appeared, it used up a lot of computer time. It consumed an equal amount of human time as well. Users played Adventure, often late into the evening, until they could solve *all* of its puzzles. It was an easy game to be obsessive about. Sessions could be saved and reloaded, so individual adventures might go on for days or weeks or longer. Generally, it takes a minimum of two weeks for a dedicated player to become a master adventurer. Usually longer.

COMPUTER SPELUNKING

What has rarely been acknowledged about Adventure is that for many years it was one of the best ways for new users to overcome their fear of the computer. The computer has little tolerance for ambiguity. Adventure also demands precision in thought and execution. Properly used, a computer rewards. Properly played, so does Adventure. Once a person has experienced the wonders of the Colossal Cave, he or she is then ready for the greatest text-mode adventure of all, the operating system. That's where your spelunking experience *really* pays off.

No college or company ever successfully banned Adventure, though many tried. At some installations, the game was modified so it could only be played during nonworking hours, nights and weekends primarily. Some versions of Adventure also had a time-limit per game session.

Eventually, however, as the various adventurers found their way to the last puzzle in the game, the mania would pass and business would return to something resembling normal. Except that those who had been down into the Colossal Cave didn't quite *talk* the same anymore. There were new words and phrases in their vocabularies. It's no accident that many computer terms are adventure-derived. (Doesn't everybody have a local wizard to call for computer assistance?)

By the end of the seventies, the personal computer revolution had begun in earnest, and almost as fast as those first machines moved into the homes of hobbyists and programmers, so did Adventure. The migration was inevitable.

At first, porting the game over seemed an almost impossible programming challenge. Most of those early machines had a maximum of 64K of memory. No more was possible. And floppy disks were limited to 90K of storage space! (There were no such things as hard drives for personal computers yet.) Those programmers who thought only in terms of mainframes, where the entire program had to be stored in memory to run, were certain that the task of porting Adventure to a microcomputer was impossible. At more than 300K, Adventure was just *too large* for a 64K machine.

Nevertheless, like an unstoppable virus, Adventure found a way in.

The trick, as more than one clever programmer figured out, was to put the program on one floppy disk and the data files on another. (Remember, this was in the days before hard disks.) The program didn't have to store *all* of the long, detailed room descriptions in the computer's memory; it could read each description off a floppy when it was needed. Really clever programmers tokenized as much of the text as possible, further reducing the demands on memory and disk space. Most of these first efforts worked fast enough to make the home versions of Adventure as playable as any mainframe version. Eventually, implementations of Adventure appeared for almost every machine on the market, and several of them evolved into powerful gaming engines on which many other adventure-type games were based. Ultimately, there were dozens of translations, including one ambitious one written in BASIC and published in David Ahl's *Creative Computing* magazine.

CLASSIC ADVENTURE

The original – the *classic* version – of the Colossal Cave Adventure had (approximately) 130 locations and required you to earn a score of 350 points to become a Master Adventurer. Some time during the late seventies, David Platt of Honeywell's Los Angeles Development Center rewrote the game, expanding the cave to 200 locations and a maximum of 550 points. This version, called Enhanced Adventure or Expanded Adventure, was installed on many networks, including GEnie and CompuServe. A somewhat different version was installed on the (now defunct) Source, but it is no longer available anywhere.

Both the Original Adventure and the Enhanced Adventure are now in the public domain, although individual implementations may be copyrighted to specific programmers.

The largest known cave is Humongous Cave, from Dave Malmberg, which has 300 locations, over 200 creatures and puzzles, and a total possible score of 1,000 points. The Humongous Cave is a further expansion of David Platt's 550-point version.

For the truly obsessive, we have included all three of these versions of Adventure. You can start with the original and work your way up. Or you can go straight to the Humongous Cave, and you'll probably never be heard from again.

How to Play Adventure

You play the game by typing one- or two-word commands. If the game understands what you want, it responds appropriately. If it doesn't understand, it will say, "I don't understand that," or simply, "Huh?"

```
> WEST
You are at the west end of Hall of Mists. A low wide crawl continues west and another goes north. To
the south is a little passage 6 feet off the floor.

> WEST
You are at the east end of a very long hall apparently without side chambers. To the east a low wide
crawl slants up. To the north a round two foot hole slants down.

> WEST
You are at the west end of a very long featureless hall. The hall joins up with a narrow north/south
passage.

> WEST
There is no way to go that direction. You're at the west end of the Long Hall.
```

If you've made it this far, you're probably hooked; you're not only in the Long Hall, you're in for the *long haul.*

This is a large part of the charm of Adventure. Every so often, you stumble across a bit of trickery or a play on words that leaves you both groaning and laughing. Congratulations on bringing light to the dark room. Watch out for the barren room. You are in a twisty little maze....

The Colossal Cave seems to go on forever. Each new move takes you deeper and deeper into the bowels of the Earth. Many of the rooms contain treasures for the taking; others have mysterious objects which you might need later. Some rooms give you magic words with which you can teleport yourself back to the starting point and leave your treasures there. There's a limit to how much you can carry, you see.

Word Lists

Adventure recognizes several hundred words. Part of the fun is discovering what words the game recognizes and what happens when you enter different commands. Nevertheless, if you're a first-time adventurer, you might find it helpful to have a list to refer to.

Two files in the subdirectory \CHAP01\HINTS will provide the verbs (ADV_VERB.TXT) and nouns (ADV_NOUN.TXT) the original Adventure recognizes. These lists are only for the 350-point original Adventure. The expanded games recognize even *more* words. To view the files, you can use the DOS TYPE command. If you want to see the list of verbs, go to the subdirectory where the files are stored and enter TYPE ADV_VERB.TXT ¦ MORE.

Which Original Adventure?

When we started to put this collection together, we found we had over a dozen different versions of Original Adventure to choose from, clearly, an embarrassment of riches.

While all of the implementations were essentially the same game, there were still enough differences to give us pause. Which version came closest to the look and feel of the original? Which version was the most playable? Should we go for historical accuracy or playability?

Most of the games had minor differences in the text. One version had an extra object at the beginning that was not in the original game. Several came with source code. The most playable game had an expanded parser which recognized additional words and allowed multiple commands on a single line. We honestly couldn't decide which of these games was the best one to represent the original Colossal Cave Adventure.

So . . . we decided to include different implementations that we found interesting. We had the space on disc, and we thought you'd appreciate seeing some of the different ways that Adventure has been translated over the years.

Original Adventure

by Don Ekman

This is the late Don Ekman's famous port to DOS of the original FORTRAN source code for Adventure (see Figure 1-1). (This is the game that David M. Bagget used as the source for CCR.EXE.) This is as historically accurate a version of the game as you are likely to find anywhere.

Most modern implementations of Adventure use normal text, with both caps and lowercase, which is considerably easier to read than all caps. You may find this game historically interesting, but uncomfortable to play for very long.

On the plus side, this version has a wizard mode, which allows you to set the hours and days when it can be played. Were it not for the fact that there are so many unrestricted and enhanced versions of Adventure easily available now, this would be an excellent feature for network installations. Nevertheless, it's still interesting to see how the wizard mode worked in the original.

Of much more *immediate* use is an ancillary file called WALKTHRU.ADV. This is a list of commands that should take you through the entire game, all the way to a 350-point triumph. You will have to make allowances for murderous dwarves and thieving pirates, of course.

Directory: \CHAP01\ADVENTUR
To Play: **ADVENT.EXE**
Date: 8-4-91
Archive: ADVENT.ZIP
Registration: $0

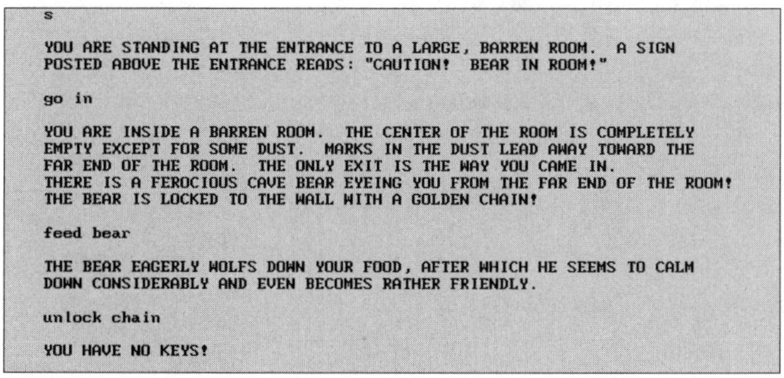

Figure 1-1
ADVENT.EXE
A grizzly experience.

Colossal Cave Revisited

by David M. Bagget

Colossal Cave Revisited (Figure 1-2) is a very playable implementation of Adventure with several useful improvements. You can put multiple commands on a single line, separated by the word "and" or a comma. The parser will process each command in turn, stopping only if it comes to a command it doesn't understand. The parser also understands the words "all" and "except," so you can "take all" or "drop all except ..." if necessary. There are times when you will appreciate this convenience. (Read the documentation for other playing tips.) One particularly nice touch, the game annotates the number of points you gain or lose by specific actions.

When you quit the game, it invites you to "Come back and visit the newly remodeled Colossal Cave soon!" This may lead you to believe that the game has been substantially modified; however, it is not the game, but the interface that has been remodeled.

Directory: CHAP01\CCR
To Play: **CCR.EXE**
Date: 7-10-93
Archive: CCR.ZIP
Registration: $0

Contact: ADVENTIONS
P. O. Box 851
Columbia, MD 21044

Cave

by Dave Malmberg

You'll hear a lot about the Adventure Game Toolkit in this book. It's quite a package, as Cave (see Figure 1-3) demonstrates. One of the things that often slows down adventure-game authors is having to write and debug the game engine before they can ever write the game itself. The Adventure Game Toolkit provides a complete

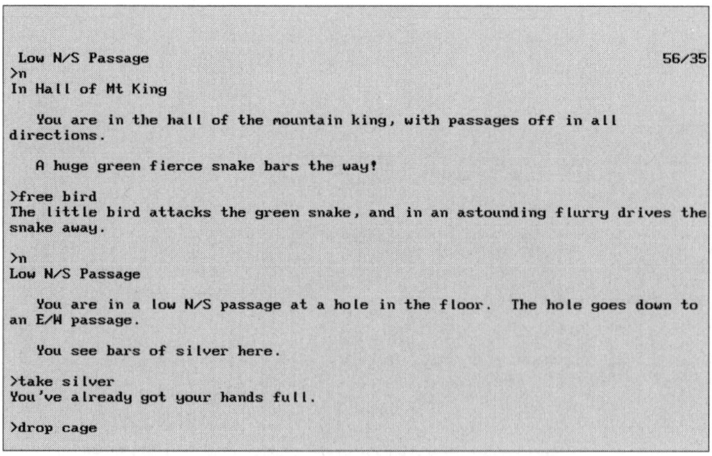

Figure 1-2
COLOSSAL CAVE REVISITED
The bird can be very useful.

system for writing, compiling, and running adventure games. Many talented game authors have written some very sophisticated games using the AGT, and we've included several of the best in this collection.

As a bonus, the AGT compiler also comes with the complete source code for the original Colossal Cave Adventure. This is the compiled code, and it is an excellent introduction to AGT's very effective interface and game engine. The engine is the RUN.EXE file. To run the game, you enter **RUN CAVE** or simply **CAVE**. (The CAVE.BAT file contains the "RUN CAVE" command.)

AGT's parser lets you put multiple commands on a single line, separated by the word "and" or a comma. The game will process each command in turn, stopping only if it comes to a command it doesn't understand. This implementation also understands the word "all." This is a useful convenience.

Another nice touch, the AGT engine lets you set the screen colors for the game. Simply change the first line of the CAVE.TTL file, where the colors are specified with the COLORS command.

By the way, you'll notice an extra object in the little building, a metallic cloak. While this isn't authentic to the original game, it does help slow down the knives of bloodthirsty dwarves. (If a dwarf throws an axe at you, throw it back.) There are other minor changes in the text of the game, but all in keeping with the original spirit. As a result, this version of Adventure seems "friendlier" than most others.

Directory: \CHAP01\CAVE
To Play: **CAVE.BAT**
Date: 5-2-93
Archive: CAVE-S.ZIP
Registration: freeware

```
 "Y2"                                              SCORE: 55      MOVE: 79
and a wall of broken rock to the east.  There is a large "Y2" on a rock in the
room's center.

What Now? PLUGH

As you say the magic word, you are instantly transported to ...
You are inside a building, a well house for a large spring.  The stream
bubbles up out of the ground and flows out the side of the building through a
pair of 1 foot diameter sewer pipes.

What Now? DROP COINS, DROP SILVER

You drop the rare coins.

You drop the silver bars.

What Now? PLUGH

As you say the magic word, you are instantly transported to ...
You are in a large room, with a passage to the south, a passage to the west,
and a wall of broken rock to the east.  There is a large "Y2" on a rock in the
room's center.

What Now?
```

Figure 1-3
CAVE (Adventure Game Toolkit)
Here's a quick way to bring your treasures home.

EXPANDING THE CAVE

In the late seventies, the Colossal Cave was expanded and extensively remodeled. David Platt added 70 new rooms, raising the total possible score to 550 points. He worked from the original FORTRAN code. His additions maintained the original spirit of the game and were well received by gamers.

Expanded Adventure spread through the ARPAnet from one DEC system to the next, just as fast as the Original Adventure, and with the same kind of impact. Old-timers came back to the cave to see what had been added, and thousands of new players were caught up in the excitement too. Expanded Adventure migrated quickly to the PC world and has been a staple of shareware collections ever since. Many users now consider the 550-point version to be the *definitive* Adventure.

Adventure 550

This implementation of Expanded Adventure (see Figure 1-4) is in the public domain. The documentation explains that it was ported from a DEC PDP-11 system and converted to work with Microsoft FORTRAN. Because the game was distributed freely in DEC-land through the DEC user society, this version has likewise been made available for free distribution in the PC world. Unfortunately, the accompanying documentation is sparse.

The game itself is authentic to its source, and is probably the most commonly available version of Adventure in circulation (classic *or* expanded).

The parser is a simple one. It does not accept the word "all," but it will accept multiple commands on a line. There are sixteen magic words in this version of Adventure. You will need to use them all to escape the cylindrical room. (There's a saved game in the archive, which puts you in the cylindrical room so you can test your theories of escape.)

If you get stuck, and you probably will, take a look at the SOLUTION.ADV file in the archive, which walks you through the major puzzles of the game.

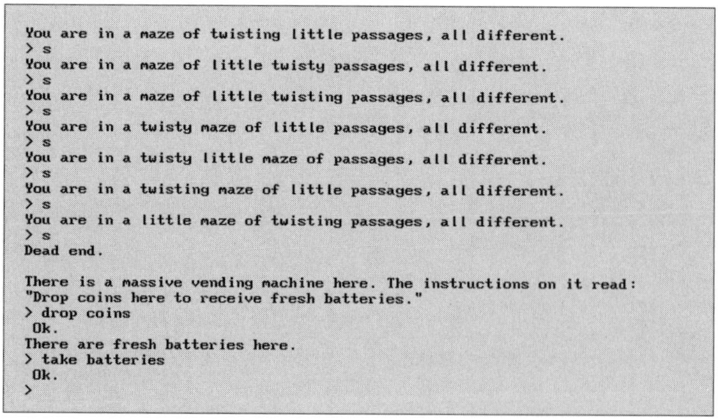

Figure 1-4
ADVENTURE 550
Getting out again is another problem.

Directory: \CHAP01\550
To Play: **ADV.EXE**
Date: 6-27-87
Archive: ADV550.ZIP

THE HUMONGOUS CAVE

The Colossal Cave continues to expand. It is now the *Humongous Cave*.

Prior versions of the cave were developed first in the mainframe world of Unix and FORTRAN and then ported over. Humongous Cave is something of a landmark because it is the first major evolution of Adventure to come from the world of MS-DOS.

Written in the Adventure Game Toolkit, Humongous Cave has a top score of *one thousand* points! It is one of the largest Adventures ever written. It has an extensive map, many amazing puzzles, and some fascinating treasures.

If you're an Adventure purist, you might find some parts of the Humongous Cave a little bit over the top. There are surprise appearances by everyone from the Internal Revenue Service to the robot from *Lost In Space*. But most of the additions are delightful surprises, and well in keeping with the freewheeling spirit of the original Adventure.

By now, of course, so many hundreds of thousands, perhaps millions, of gamers have been through the Colossal Cave that it's no longer a cave, it's a theme park. The cave has obviously grown to meet the demands of popularity, adding all these new attractions to please its increasing numbers of visitors.

In its next incarnation, the little building at the end of the road will probably be a ticket booth. You'll find a two-hour waiting line at the locked grate, a Pirates of the Caribbean ride in the twisty little maze, and hordes of tourists with camcorders at the Magnificent View, all enjoying another Kodak moment. You'll need an E-ticket to kill the Dragon. (Hmm. Maybe I'll write that version myself.)

Will there be any more expansions of Adventure? Some adventurers feel that the cave has gotten as large as it can without becoming unplayable. Humongous Cave is no longer a game, it's a career.

But it would certainly be premature to write an end to the Colossal Cave Adventure. It seems more likely that the cave will be luring cyberspace spelunkers for many years to come. As long as there are adventurers, there will probably be explorers adding new sections to the cave.

HugeCave: Adventure in Humongous Cave

by Dave Malmberg

Adventure in Humongous Cave (see Figure 1-5) is not only the largest version of the Colossal Cave, it is the largest adventure ever written.

Based on the 550-point Expanded Adventure, which in turn was based on the 350-point Original Adventure, the Humongous Cave is the ultimate evolution of the classic game.

The Humongous Cave has 300 locations and 200 creatures, treasures, and puzzles. The game is full of delicious surprises. Some of them are hilarious. But don't laugh too

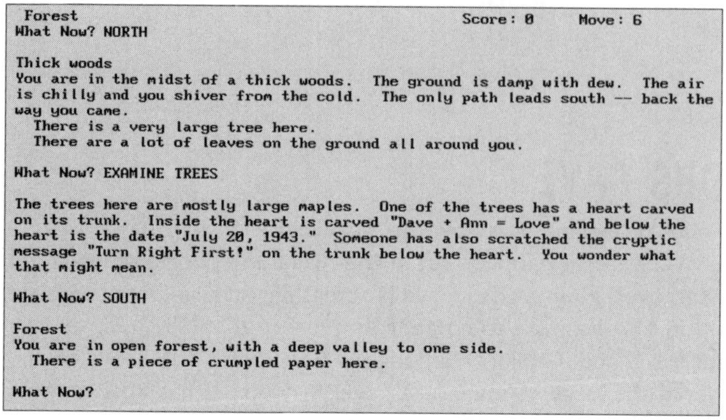

Figure 1-5
HUGECAVE
Is this information helpful? Is it safe?

hard, the joke might be on you. This is a tough game to solve. Some of the puzzles are amazingly frustrating, which may be exactly what you want in a game like this, but at 3:00 in the morning, you might find yourself wondering if it really is all that important to figure out what the rabbit's foot is good for and why your treasures keep disappearing when you bring them back to the little building. After all, it's only a game, isn't it? You should have been more careful when you stumbled into the programmer's den.

Written with the Adventure Game Toolkit, the game has a very playable interface. AGT's parser lets you put multiple commands on a single line, separated by the word "and" or a comma. The game processes each command in turn, stopping only if it comes to a command it doesn't understand. The game understands the word "all" and using it does speed up play.

Extensive documentation is included here. The HUGECAVE.WLK file includes a complete history of Adventure, very detailed instructions on how to play the game, and a complete walk-through solution of the Humongous Cave.

An extra bonus is the POPHINT module that comes with the Humongous Cave. At any time during play, press ALT-H. (Press the ALT key and the H key at the same time.) This will bring up the hint utility which can help you get through the more difficult parts of the cave.

HUGECAVE needs 512K of free memory. If you also use the POPHINT module, your system will need 532K. Most computer systems should be able to handle this, but it's possible that you may have some memory-hogging device drivers installed. In that case, you'll have to change your memory configuration to get HUGECAVE to run. (Check your DOS manual.)

Directory: \CHAP01\HUGECAVE
To Play: **HUGECAVE.BAT**
HINTCAVE.BAT (to use POPHINT module)
Date: 1-9-94
Archive: HUGECAVE.ZIP
Registration: freeware

Hints

The Colossal Cave Adventure has two particularly frustrating mazes. One is a maze of twisty little passages all alike. The other is a maze of twisting little passages, all different. It's very easy to get stuck in either of these traps. It's almost impossible to escape without a map.

The best way to map the mazes is to drop one object in each room, then keep moving around, mapping the relationships, until you've identified which room leads to which.

If that doesn't help, or if you're too impatient, then you can use one of the two hint maps we've provided on the CD-ROM.

Directory: \CHAP01\HINTS
To View: **TYPE MAZE1.TXT | MORE**
To View: **TYPE MAZE2.TXT | MORE**
Archive: ADVHINTS.ZIP

Under slightly different names, these two files have been floating around BBS systems for several years. There are no author's credits for either map, but there are countless adventurers who are certainly grateful to have them.

THE GREAT UNDERGROUND EMPIRE!

```
Dungeon is a game of adventure, danger, and low cunning. In it you will explore some of the most
amazing territory ever seen by mortal man. Hardened adventurers have run screaming from the terrors
contained within.
```

The Colossal Cave adventure was only the first. Like any great work, it had such a tremendous impact on its audience that it inspired other authors to create their own adventures. In the mid-seventies, two students at the Programming Technology Division of the M.I.T. Computer Science Laboratory, Mark Blank and Dave Lebling, began to create their own underground empire.

From the very first, it was their goal to do something extraordinary. They wanted to allow the computer to understand more common English sentences than the limited and sometimes frustrating two-word parser of the Colossal Cave Adventure. Toward that end, Mark Blank created ZIL, the Zork Interactive Language. ZIL was built around a parser that allowed the program to find associations between sentences so it could better understand what the player wanted to do.

Dungeon was so popular as a mainframe adventure that eventually Lebling and Blank went commercial with it, forming a company called Infocom to market the game for home computers. The commercial version was called Zork and it sold hundreds of thousands of copies for Apple, CP/M, and eventually MS-DOS machines. Zork was the first game of a long line of popular adventures using the Zork engine, and it helped make Infocom the most successful adventure-game publisher of the eighties. Zork also spawned two sequels, Zork II and Zork III.

The original game, Dungeon, has long since been released to the public domain. There are (at least) two versions of it available for MS-DOS computers. As there is no significant difference between them, we have included only one of them here.

Dungeon

by Tim Anderson, Marc Blank, Bruce Daniels, and Dave Lebling

When you begin this game, you are standing next to a mailbox. If you open the mailbox, you'll find a leaflet telling you some of the history of the game. Dungeon (Figure 1-6) was inspired by the Colossal Cave Adventure, as well as by the Dungeons and Dragons role-playing games.

What the leaflet doesn't tell you is that Dungeon is as much a classic as the Colossal Cave, and has inspired the same kind of obsessive enthusiasm from gamers everywhere. The descriptions are evocative, the puzzles are clever, and the sly humor of the game adds a delicious sense of fun. Watch out for the thief. He's every bit as annoying as the pirate in the Colossal Cave perhaps even more so, he's a much more talented adversary.

The commercial version of Dungeon, called Zork: The Great Underground Empire, has been a favorite for many years, as have both the sequels, Zork II and Zork III. Return to Zork, a multimedia adventure with spectacular graphics, is proving itself equally popular among modern gamers. If you like Dungeon, you're sure to like the rest of the Zork sequels. You should be able to find them in most well-stocked computer software outlets.

Because Dungeon exists as freeware in the mainframe world, this translation of it to the MS-DOS arena has also been made public domain.

Directory:	\CHAP01\DUNGEON
To Play:	**DUNGEON.EXE**
Date:	9-24-87
Archive:	DUNGEON.ZIP

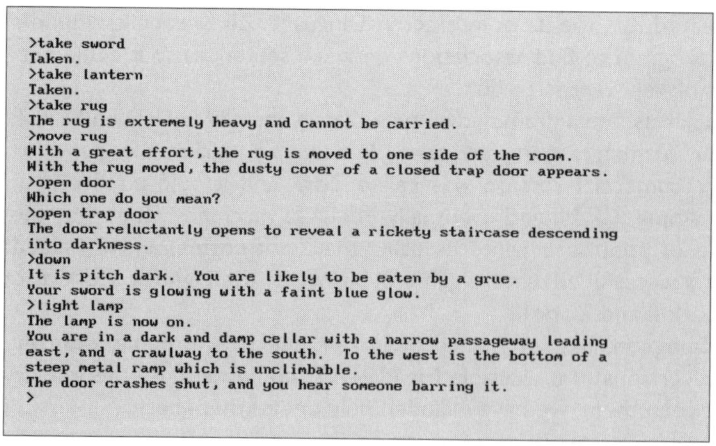
```
>take sword
Taken.
>take lantern
Taken.
>take rug
The rug is extremely heavy and cannot be carried.
>move rug
With a great effort, the rug is moved to one side of the room.
With the rug moved, the dusty cover of a closed trap door appears.
>open door
Which one do you mean?
>open trap door
The door reluctantly opens to reveal a rickety staircase descending
into darkness.
>down
It is pitch dark.  You are likely to be eaten by a grue.
Your sword is glowing with a faint blue glow.
>light lamp
The lamp is now on.
You are in a dark and damp cellar with a narrow passageway leading
east, and a crawlway to the south.  To the west is the bottom of a
steep metal ramp which is unclimbable.
The door crashes shut, and you hear someone barring it.
>
```

Figure 1-6
DUNGEON
The point of no return?

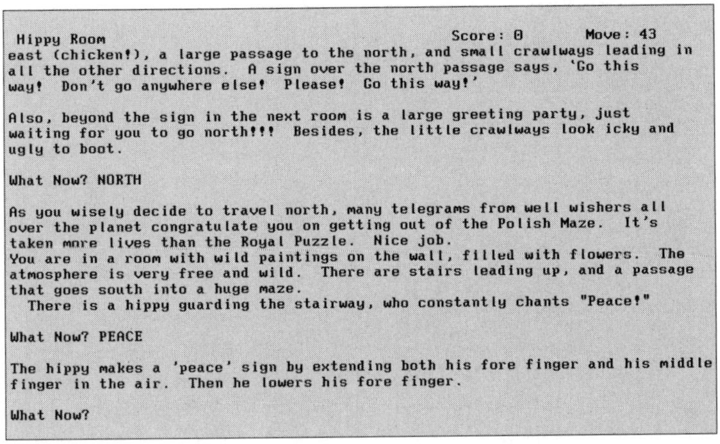

Figure 1-7
PORK I
The dreaded Polish Maze claims another victim.

Pork 1: The Great Underground Sewer System

by Dave Malmberg

Pork I (shown in Figure 1-7) is a parody of Zork I, The Great Underground Empire, but you don't need to have played Zork to enjoy this satire. Previous experience with Zork might give you some useful clues, but don't count on it.

Pork I was written with the Adventure Game Toolkit. Although the documentation says that this is a betatest of a new version of the AGT, the game itself is quite rugged, as is the underlying game engine. You shouldn't experience any problems.

If you are a Zork enthusiast, then this is a must-have game. Even if you're not a dedicated Zork player, you're going to find this a lot of fun. This is an inspired parody. (If you get stuck or trapped, the PORK.SOL file contains a walk-through of the entire game.)

Directory: \CHAP01\PORK1
To Play: **PORK1.BAT**
Date: 8-19-91
Archive: PORK15.ZIP

Pork 2: The Gizzard of Showbiz

by Bill Larkins

Continuing the tradition, Pork 2 (see Figure 1-8) is a parody of Zork II, Infocom's second Zork adventure. Your familiarity with the Zork universe may help you here. Then again, it may not. In either case, you will be entertained by the not-too-gentle roasting of a classic adventure game.

Pork 2 was written with the Adventure Game Toolkit. You'll find it as easy to play as all the other adventures that use AGT's engine. The game comes with no additional documentation, except what you can find as you proceed through your adventure. By now, however, you shouldn't need much help. The bad news is that the game does not

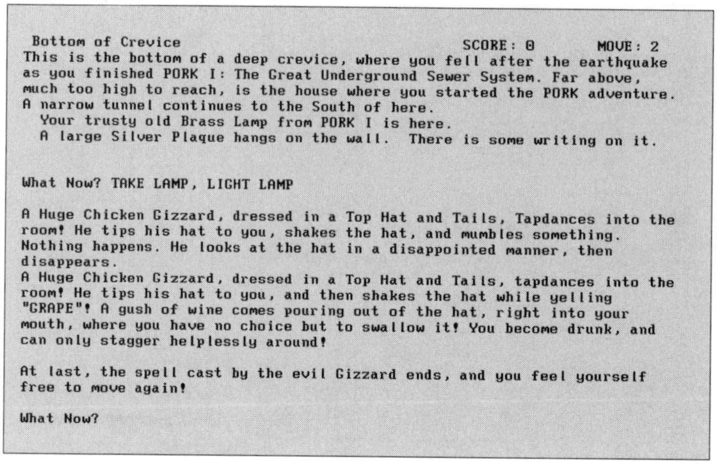

Figure 1-8
PORK 2
When good games go weird. . . .

come with a walk-through solution, so you're on your own here. If you get *really* stuck, however, the source code is available in the CompuServe GAMERS forum.

This adventure does have one interesting aspect not seen in many other games. It has a *lewd* mode. At any point in the game, you may enter the command "lewd." The game will then ask you a question, the answer to which you are only likely to know if you are over twenty-one. If the lewd mode is too much for you, you can always enter the command "tame."

As with Pork 1, if you are a Zork enthusiast, then this is a must-have game, and even if you're not a Zork player, this is still a very clever adventure.

Directory: \CHAP01\PORK2
To Play: **PORK2.BAT**
Date: 1-22-89
Archive: PORK2A.ZIP
Registration: $0

Contact: Bill Larkins
Internet: larkins@CPUG.ORG

CHAPTER 2

DUNGEONS

DUNGEONS

Eventually, of course, adventurers wanted pictures. In the early days of PCs, there were no graphics. What you had were 25 rows and 80 columns of text characters. This gave you a playing field of 2,000 screen locations, and 128 possible characters. Prior to the PC, you couldn't even be sure of 25 rows or 80 columns, let alone the full range of ASCII characters.

Even when CGA video cards became commonplace, available graphics were still crude and ugly. There was little to challenge the imagination.

Enter Rogue.

Rogue demonstrated that the conditions of the text-mode environment did not have to limit the imagination, but could challenge it instead. Rogue combined role-playing adventure with text-mode graphics and on-screen auto-mapping. As you moved through the maze, exploring the passages, rooms, and levels, the map drew itself around you. Everything was represented by letters and symbols, but the more you played, the deeper you fell into the reality of the Dungeon of Doom.

Your challenge was to travel all the way down to the bottom-most level and retrieve the powerful Amulet of Yendor! There would be strange and terrible monsters to battle, new ones on every level. There was gold to be found and treasures to be won. Most exciting, *every game was different.* Rogue generated new levels of the dungeon on the fly. Every time you went down the stairs, the game created a fresh new maze.

Just as the Colossal Cave Adventure and Zork began in the world of mainframes running Unix, so did Rogue, and later on, its descendants, Hack and Nethack. And just like the Colossal Cave and Zork, Rogue also inspired a number of imitations.

Of course, it's no accident that some of the very best games began in the mainframe world and migrated over to PCs. The mainframes were the first machines to have the speed and memory necessary to create playable environments. The Unix machines were already two generations ahead, so they were a great playground for programmers. And because many of those mainframes were linked to a nationwide network (the ARPAnet which later became the Internet), game designers often received immediate feedback on their efforts, plus lots of suggestions from enthusiasts on what to add in the next release. This made the Unix world a much more productive arena for serious gamers, and it stayed that way for a long time.

Once those same gamers started putting PCs on their desks, they brought their toys over too – to the benefit of all of us.

CASTLE

by Kevin Bales

You are trapped in a deserted Castle and you must escape. It is rumored that the castle is full of treasures. Can you find them all?
Use the cursor keypad to move your man around the rooms. To pick up a visible item, just run into it. To pick up an item not displayed on the screen, use the command GET. To attack monsters just run into them, but only if you have a weapon. The computer accepts most two-word commands. There are 83 rooms & 13 treasures. To see the High Score, look at the wall in the courtyard. One hint: Look at everything carefully!

Castle (see Figure 2-1) is an under-acknowledged landmark in the history of MS-DOS programming. It was the first attempt to do a graphic adventure game *on the PC*. In fact, for quite some time it was the only graphic adventure game. Despite the simplicity of its imagery, it grabbed the imagination of its audience.

If you're running a fast machine, you might want to run a slowdown utility before you play Castle.

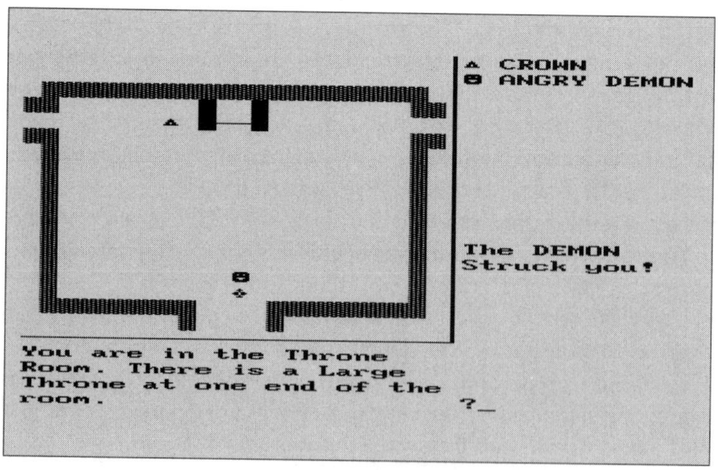

Figure 2-1
CASTLE
The first graphic adventure for the PC.

Directory: \CHAP02\CASTLE
To Play: **CASTLE.EXE**
Date: 3-18-85
Archive: CASTLE.ZIP
Registration: $10 contribution

Contact: Kevin Bales
1250 Lindenwood Lane
Atlanta, GA 30319

ROGUE: THE DUNGEONS OF DOOM

originated by Michael C. Toy and Kenneth C.R.C. Arnold
adapted for MS-DOS by Jon Lane
significant design contributions by Glenn Wichman and scores of others

Rogue is a legendary game. It is a landmark. It is the granddaddy of all dungeons. Why? Because it was the first of a whole new kind of game.

Rogue, shown in Figure 2-2, is both a role-playing adventure and a maze-exploration game. It uses text-mode "graphics" for on-screen auto-mapping. There are 26 different monster types, each one represented by a different letter of the alphabet, and 26 different levels. You will encounter a different selection of monsters on each level. Despite the simplicity of the graphics, the cumulative effect is quite persuasive.

In Rogue, you are a thief. Your goal is to make your way to the lowest level of the maze and steal the mysterious and powerful Amulet of Yendor! As you go, you will find armor and weapons, treasures of various kinds, and a wide variety of magical potions, spells, wands, and rings. You will have to learn how to use all of these by experimentation. Of particular interest, the game creates its levels as you play, generating each new maze as needed. This means that no two games are alike.

By comparison with its sequels, Hack and Nethack, Rogue is a relatively simple implementation. Nevertheless, some players prefer the simplicity of Rogue, and it remains a classic. Although Rogue is copyrighted to Epyx Games, there were a number of public domain releases from 1983 to 1986. We have chosen to include the final public domain release of Rogue. (Press V to see the version number. It will report that this is the public doman release. Press F1 for the list of other options.)

Note: Before you run Rogue, use a text editor to modify the ROGUE.OPT file for your system. The ROGUE.OPT file lets you tell Rogue what drive you are running it from. Otherwise, the game could hang up your system. ROGUE.OPT also lets you set other parameters. Fortunately, it's self-documenting. Just read it for instructions.

As an extra bonus, we've also tracked down the game manual which has not been included in most shareware distributions. ROGUE.MAN was written by two of the authors of the game, Michael C. Toy and Kenneth C.R.C. Arnold, and it will tell you everything you need to know about Rogue.

Oh, one more thing. Be sure to kiss your family goodbye before you start playing this game. It may be several months before you see them again.

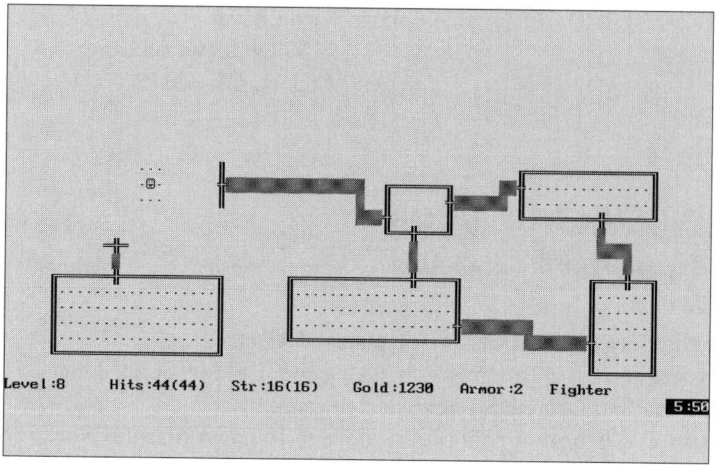

Figure 2-2
ROGUE
Sometimes you're in the dark...

Directory: \CHAP02\ROGUE
To Play: **ROGUE.EXE**
Date: 2-4-86
Archive: ROGUE.ZIP
Registration: public domain

We've also included a good collection of hint files written by experienced gamers in the subdirectory \CHAP02\ROGUE\HINTS. Although these are not official documentation files, they do provide a lot of useful information.

Directory: \CHAP02\ROGUE\HINTS
File: ROGUE.NOT (Useful if you're having trouble making the game work)

ROGUE.HNT (A list of the 26 different monsters)

ROGUE.HLP (A very detailed explanation of how the various magic bits work, and how to use them most effectively)

ROGUE.DOC (A general overview, not comprehensive, but still very useful)

ROGUE.TXT (This file is actually about the Atari version of the game, but almost all of it is applicable to the MS-DOS version too. This file is so comprehensive and so well written that it's well worth your attention.)

ROGUE.FAQ (A list of frequently asked questions and answers.)

Setting up Hack and Nethack

Hack can be a little tricky to install, because the authors of the game have assumed that you know your way around a computer. This can be an intimidating assumption especially if you're used to programs that search out the capabilities of your system and automatically configure themselves. Hack isn't one of these.

Nevertheless, it's possible to set up Hack very quickly. Simply create a \HACK subdirectory on your C: drive, and \SAVE and \LEVELS subdirectories within the ..\HACK subdirectory. Copy all of the Hack files into the C:\HACK subdirectory, and you're ready to play.

If you want to put Hack on another drive or in another directory, use a text editor to alter three lines in the HACK.CNF file. Don't panic. The file is self-documenting; it contains explanations of what you're doing. You'll want to change the HACKDIR=, SAVE=, and LEVELS= lines to indicate which directories will be storing the specific files. You can set other options in the HACK.CNF file too, including your name, the kind of character you're playing, whether or not to automatically pick up everything you pass over, and what graphics characters to use on-screen.

Generally, you'll find that Hack, whichever version you're playing, is fairly well documented. There's always a README file containing the most important information you need to know to get started, and there are usually other files to help you play.

Getting into Hack might take a little more effort than you're used to, but it's worth it.

HACK

1.03 by Jay Fenlason, Kenny Woodland, Mike Thome, and John Payne
major rewrite by Andries Brouwer
ported to the PC by Don G. Kneller
3.6 by Don G. Kneller

Rogue was only the beginning. Inspired by Rogue, Jay Fenlason began creating a role-playing dungeon of his own, one with even more monsters and levels. He called it Hack. Other progammers joined him and Hack became a shared creation, comprising the best ideas of all of them. The game remains one of the most lively and playable adventures ever constructed, and it remains in active development even to this day.

Most of the changes between 1.03 (shown in Figure 2-3) and 3.6 (seen in Figure 2-4) were added features to the playing engine and bug-fixes. Release 3.6 is much more playable and rugged, but it is also noteworthy because it was the first version to add significant changes to the content of the game itself. You'll discover the differences when you play.

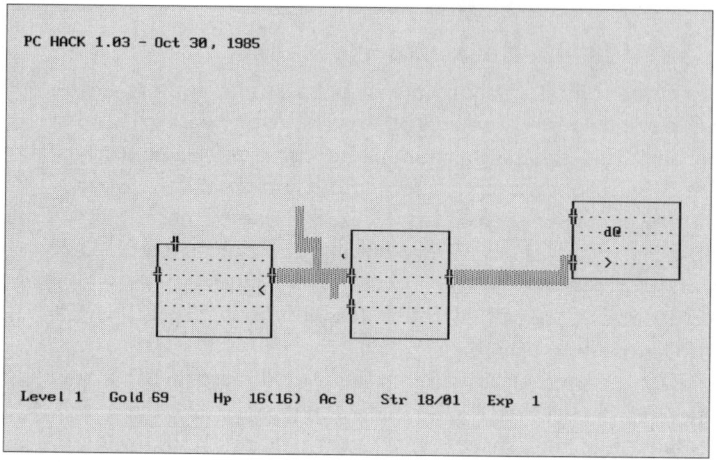

Figure 2-3
HACK 1.03
It only looks simple.

On the surface, Hack looks a lot like Rogue. If you know how to play one, you know how to play the other, but the deeper you go in Hack, the more it will surprise you. Where Rogue has only 26 monsters, Hack has twice as many critters, because it uses both uppercase and lowercase letters to represent its menagerie. The expanded repertoire of beasties includes floating eyes, snakes, gnomes, orcs, owlbears, giant ants, giant spiders, acid blobs, trappers, piercers, centaurs (which are especially hard to kill), jaguars, tengus, leprechauns, and killer bees. The killer bees are the worst; they just keep coming and coming and coming.

But at least this time, you're not alone. On your side, there's a friendly little dog, represented by a "d," to keep you company and help you fight battles. The little dog will even pick up (or steal from a shopkeeper) useful items for you. You'll find that the little dog has a very independent personality, but if you have a whistle, you can call him back to you if he roams too far.

Hack also gives you a much wider selection of armor to wear and weapons to wield, not to mention all the new wands to wave, potions to quaff, spells to read, and rings to wear. The wands, spells, potions, and rings are rarely identified. The program reassigns powers and attributes every time you start a new game, so you have to test each item to identify what it does. You cannot win the game without a full bag of tools.

Much more than Rogue, Hack is a role-playing game. The emphasis is not on solving specific puzzles within a structured framework, but on using the tools of your chosen identity to cope with different situations.

You can play Hack as a knight, a fighter, a caveman, a wizard, a speleologist, or a tourist. The role you choose will affect what kinds of weapons and tools you find as you descend. A wizard will find more wands and spells than a knight. A knight will find more weapons. And along the way, you will find lots of gold which you can spend at the conveniently located shops within the dungeon. The kind of merchandise you find also seems to reflect the role you're playing. Like any good role-playing game, Hack also

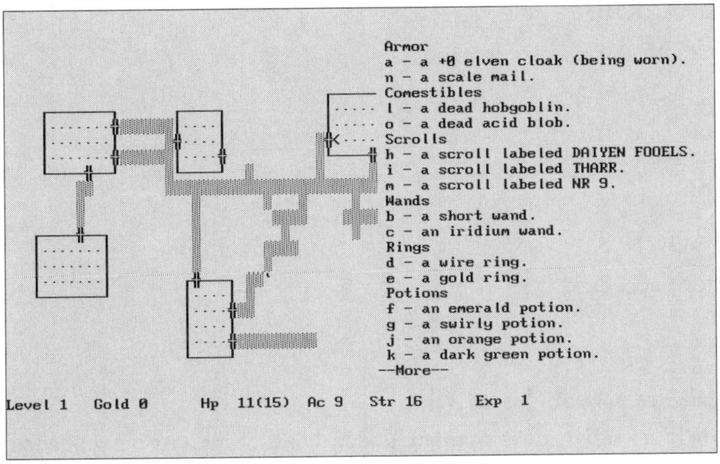

Figure 2-4
HACK 3.6
You are carrying a lot more than you think.

keeps track of personal statistics, and this is reflected by the status line at the bottom of the screen showing health, wealth, experience points, experience level, number of turns, hit points, strength, and hunger level.

Like Rogue, a new level is generated each time you go down the stairs, and each new level is just a little bit harder than the one before. You will encounter ever more difficult opponents, so you're going to have to keep testing the capabilities of your weapons and your magic to expand your repertoire of responses. Sometimes, however, Hack does not generate a new level. If you get killed, there's a good chance that the level will be saved so that your (now-cursed) belongings can be rediscovered the next time you reach this level. Of course, your ghost (and his dog) will be prowling around that level too; and ghosts are nearly impossible to kill, so there's another reason to be careful.

When you do find the Amulet . . . well, you'll have to fight your way back up the stairs to get it safely out of the dungeon. That's another challenge. They really don't want you to leave with it.

Ultimately, there is so much to see and do in Hack, and so many different combinations, that it's an understatement to say that no two games are alike. Even after many weeks of dedicated play, the game will continue to throw surprises at you.

Before you play, read the HACK.DOC file for instructions on how to set up the game for your specific system. It isn't difficult, just a few simple edits to the HACK.CNF so that the game will know what kind of system you're runing and where to find its files. Fortunately, HACK.CNF contains its own documentation; all you have to do is read it carefully and insert or delete a few "#" marks. Once this is done, Hack should run without problem on your machine.

Hack36 is generally regarded as the last version of Hack for the PC; after this, the game evolved into Nethack. However, as we shall see shortly, there was one more incarnation of Hack still to come.

Directory: \CHAP02\HACK103
To Play: **HACK103.EXE**
Date: 10-31-85
Archive: HACK103.ZIP

Directory: \CHAP02\HACK36
To Play: **HACK.EXE**
Date: 10-22-86
Archive: HACK36.ZIP
Registration: contributions accepted

HACKLITE

masterminded by Alan Beale and John A. Toebes VIII

Even while Nethack was in active development under Mike Stephenson's guidance, others were also working on the game, porting the code to the Amiga, recompiling it, play-testing, and taking advantage of the Amiga's excellent graphic capabilities to give Hack a whole new look.

When the Amiga version migrated back to the PC, it became Hacklite (shown in Figure 2-5). Although Hacklite has long since disappeared from most shareware distributions, it's still a lot of fun, and it does provide the experienced player with a healthy share of surprises. The most obvious difference, of course, is Hacklite's dramatic use of color. Gold is represented by yellow dollar signs, rubies are red asterisks, potions all show up in the appropriate colors, and so on. Deeper in the dungeon, you'll find that some of the inhabitants are new and some of the challenges are different from what you expect.

Hacklite also allows you to make your character death-resistant. Add "immortal" to the end of your character options; but you only get two resurrections before death is final, so don't be careless. (That's immortal with a "t," although I can't help but wonder what game behaviors an immoral option might trigger.)

For beginners, Hacklite is a little easier to configure. If your system has a color monitor and a hard disk, just copy HDCOLOR.CNF to HACKLITE.CNF and edit the file to show the game directory where Hacklite is installed. If you don't have a color monitor or a hard disk, it's time to upgrade your computer.

Directory: \CHAP02\HACKLITE
To Play: **HACKLITE.EXE**
Date: 12-4-88
Archive: HACKLITE.ZIP
Registration: $0

Contact: The Software Distillery
3750 Jamestown Circle
Raleigh, NC 27609
Internet: loiljir@squink.vvcp

Hack Hints

In the \CHAP02\HACKTIPS subdirectory, you will find five separate subdirectories, comprising one of the largest and most comprehensive sets of Hack documentation, help,

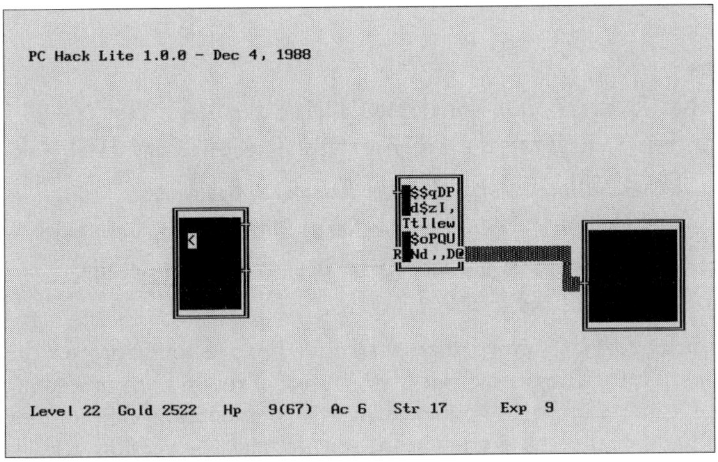

Figure 2-5
HACKLITE
Uh oh...

and hint files you're ever likely to find outside the Internet. If you get stuck in Hack, and you can't find an answer here, there isn't one.

If you have been playing for more than 100 hours and you still can't find the Amulet or kill the Wizard, then read the DONTREAD.ME file in the AMULET subdirectory. It'll help.

If you need some help getting started in the game, or some tools to help you while playing, examine the files in the HACKGIDE subdirectory. There are sample batch files and sample *.CNF files to help you get started. There is also a form you can print and fill out as you play to keep track of the powers of various wands and rings and spells. HACKGIDE.DOC also provides extensive documentation of all of the different parts of the game. It's one of the best organized and best written guides to the game you'll ever find.

In the HACKTIPS subdirectory, you'll find five separate files, each one dealing with a different aspect of the game. These are short files and well worth reading, especially if you don't feel like reading some of the more extensive files in the other subdirectories.

In the HACKTUTR subdirectory, there are three long files, containing just about everything you need to know about Hack. It's a very good introduction to the game. Plus, it also provides extensive listings of how different parts of the game work and interact in combination.

Finally, in the MORETIPS subdirectory, you'll find three useful files. There's an alternate TERMCAP file for actually running the game, plus HACK.DOC and HACK.HLP. HACK.DOC is a well-written but uncredited guide to the game, both readable and extensive. HACK.HLP is a lot of useful advice that other players have gained the hard way. For instance: don't read a scroll of genocide when you're confused. It's not healthy.

NETHACK

2.2+ by Mike Stephenson

3.0 by Mike Stephenson, Ken Arromdee, Jean-Christophe Collet, Steve Creps, Eric Hendrickson, Izchak Miller, Eric S. Raymond, John Rupley, Mike Threepoint, and Janet Walz

3.1.3 by Mike Stephenson, Izchak Miller, Janet Walz, Ken Arromdee, David Cohrs, Jean-Christophe Collet, Kevin Darcy, Matt Day, Timo Hakulinen, Steve Linhart, Dean Luick, Pat Rankin, Eric Raymond, Eric Smith, Norm Meluch, Kevin Smolkowski, Carl Schelin, Stephen Spackman, Steve VanDevender, and Paul Winner

Eventually, those who loved Hack more than they loved spare time formed the Nethack Development Team. They took Hack, which was already a mature game, and began to restructure it into a more complex gaming environment. A wealth of new material was added, and the challenges were expanded. Nethack — version 3.1.3 is shown in Figure 2.6 — is a richer and more intricate game than any of its predecessors.

Because the Nethack Development Team wants Nethack to remain portable across many different platforms, Nethack does not have flashy graphics and sound. These are usually machine-specific features, nearly impossible to implement equally on different kinds of machines. Despite this, Nethack continues to hold its place as one of the most popular games in the PC world. And beyond.

The 2.2+ release of Nethack is the version that was commonly distributed as Nethack 2. It is called 2.2+ because it has some of the features of 2.3 already incorporated. Release 2.3 apparently never made it to the MS-DOS world.

Once you start playing Nethack, some of the differences between it and its predecessor, Hack 3.6, are immediately obvious. First of all, you have a whole new range of roles to play: Do you want to be an Archeologist, a Tourist, a Barbarian, a Knight, a Caveman, a Samurai, a Ninja, a Priest, a Valkyrie, an Elf, a Healer, or a Wizard? Remember, each of these characters not only has a different range of abilities, but also a

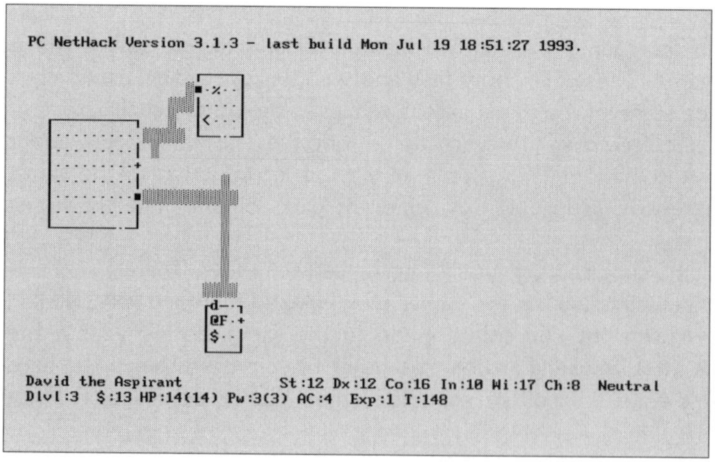

Figure 2-6
NETHACK 3.1.3
It starts out simple…

different set of tools and items available once he or she steps foot into the dungeons of doom.

The dungeons themselves have been extensively remodeled — by someone with a very weird sense of humor. The more familiar you are with previous versions of Hack, the more surprised and delighted you will be with the changes. Your little dog is still available to you, but you can always use a wand of polymorph to turn him into a tame something-or-other. Try for a tame Dragon. Those are nice. So are minotaurs.

Nethack 3.0 is a major rewrite. Again, some of the differences are immediately obvious. Doors for instance are sometimes closed, occasionally even locked. You'll need to find keys. Sometimes, instead of a little dog, you have a little kitten helping you. The kitten is represented by an "f" for feline.

Nethack 3.0 also makes much better use of color. The colors often represent the nature of an object too. Gold is represented by yellow dollar signs, emeralds are green asterisks, and fountains are blue. But Nethack 3.0 goes far behond Hacklite. By assigning different colors to letter-symbols, an even greater range of inhabitants can be created throughout the dungeon and the effect is wonderful. If you've previously been playing Hack or Nethack as a mostly monochrome game, suddenly having all this color is like being dropped into the middle of Oz. Unfortunately, there are no Munchkins to show you the fast way to the wizard. You're going to have to go downstairs, down and down and down.

The changes between Nethack 2.2+ and Nethack 3.0 are *significant.* Stop and visit an oracle. You're going to need her advice. A lot of it. The whole bottom half of the dungeon has been redesigned; it's now a world of its own with a consistent mythology throughout. You'll find that in addition to the randomly generated levels there are permanent levels, such as the Castle and Vlad's Tower that represent specific puzzles to be solved.

But Nethack 3.0 is only a warmup for Nethack 3.1.3.

Right from the very beginning, you will know that this is not the same version of Hack/Nethack that your granddad used to play. When you begin this game, you will be shown an opening screen of text that introduces you to the game, tells you of your goal, and starts you on your quest.

This is the most ambitious version of Nethack ever designed. It's no longer a game; it's a career. And I mean that in all sincerity. You could easily spend several years playing this game, testing all of its various combinations. It is here that the role-playing aspects of Hack are developed to a degree not seen in any other game, either shareware or commercial. As before, you can choose what role you want to play, but now more than ever, who you are determines the circumstances of your adventure. Tourists will not tour the same dungeon as Valkyries or Rogues. Even the sex of your character makes a difference. A female character can catch a unicorn, a male character cannot.

In this latest (but probably not final) version of Nethack, great care has been taken to create a consistent mythology throughout the dungeons. Everything interacts with everything now to a much greater degree than ever before, and you cannot win the game without knowing how to take advantage of these interactions. Even the colors of the creatures are important clues. If you're not careful, you'll even see a one-horned, one-eyed, flying purple people-eater. No kidding.

In addition to the randomly generated levels of the main dungeon, there are many *new* pieces to the game that you have never seen before — *be sure to visit the gnomish mines and pick up some lovely souvenir candles.* You should also watch out for the Rogue level. This level is modeled after those found in the original game of Rogue, the granddaddy of Nethack. It will be randomly generated. It will have exactly nine rooms, and each wall in a room may have only one exit. The level will have a different look to it, so you'll know you're someplace special.

Because many of the new levels are hard-coded instead of random, Nethack now contains specific problems to be solved, like those in a traditional adventure game. When you get to certain places, you'll need to have the right item to invoke the right spell to achieve the specific result. Be sure to check the hint files.

In short, Nethack 3.1.3 is the most elaborate role-playing environment you are ever likely to explore. This is a place to return to again and again, each time for a different experience. You're really going to have to play it for a year or two and see for yourself.

Let us know when you get back . . . *if* you get back.

Directory:	\CHAP02\NH22
To Play:	**NETHACK.EXE**
Date:	12-20-87
Archive:	NETHACK2.ZIP

Directory:	\CHAP02\NH30
To Play:	**NETHACK.EXE**
Date:	3-11-91
Archive:	NETHACK3.ZIP

Directory:	\CHAP02\NH3132 (for 286 machines)
To Play:	**NETHACK.EXE**
Date:	7-19-93
Archive:	NH3132.ZIP

Directory:	\CHAP02\NH3133 (for 386 machines or better)
To Play:	**NETHACK.EXE**
Date:	7-19-93
Archive:	NH3133.ZIP

Nethack 3.1.3 comes in two versions, one for fast, modern, expensive 386/486 computers, and one for slow, obsolete, junky-clunky, why-are-you-still-keeping-it-anyway, 286 machines. Be aware that both are very large programs. You may need to tinker with your system configuration before it will run. Check the documentation; the Nethack Team has tried to make this as easy as possible. Believe me, it's worth the effort.

Nethack Source Code

The Nethack Development Team has generously made the game's source code available for other programmers to study, test, or even modify. You'll find the PKZIP compressed files in the subdirectory \CHAP02\NH-XTRAS\CODE If you come up with an interesting patch or modification to the game, send it in to the Development Team. Who knows? You might be a part of Nethack 4.0. (Personally, I'd like to add a ring of truth that lets you know the true nature of an object, and the axe of contrition — when you hit someone with it, you make them very, very sorry.)

Directory:	\CHAP02\NH-XTRAS\CODE
Archives:	NHSRCA.ZIP
	NHSRCB.ZIP
	NHSRCC.ZIP
Date:	10-25-93

Nethack Docs

More than any other game in this collection, you're going to need the documentation for Nethack. Fortunately, there's a great deal of documentation for Nethack, both official and unofficial. We've gathered the best.

Documentation

Start with the \CHAP02\NH-XTRAS\MANUALS subdirectory. There you'll find the files FAQ.MAI, GUIDEBOO.TXT, HACK.MAN, and LICENSE.

The first document you'll find is FAQ.MAI. A FAQ is a Frequently Asked Question file. This is a semi-official document and it serves as an introduction to the game, and points you to sources for new releases and spoiler documents.

GUIDEBOO.TXT is the *official* Nethack documentation. Each individual release of Nethack comes with a guidebook, but we've included this extra copy for those readers who might have overlooked it elsewhere. (Besides, it's convenient to have all the important documentation in one place, isn't it?) This is the guidebook for Release 3.1.3 of Nethack. It should be enough to get you well into the game before you start screaming for serious help.

Additional help can be found in HACK.MAN. This is an unofficial manual that includes the material in the (previously mentioned) Hack tutorial files, but with substantial annotations and additions. Two of the new chapters specifically refer to Nethack 2.3. So if you've skipped Hack and come straight to Nethack, this is a useful overview, but be aware, it will still be insufficient for Nethack 3.0 and 3.1.3.

If neither GUIDEBOO.TXT nor HACK.MAN is sufficient, then you need to visit the \CHAP02\NH-XTRAS\SPOILERS subdirectory. Among other things, we've included the latest and most thorough spoiler file, SPOILER.700.

Finally, we're also including a copy of LICENSE, the official Nethack license. This file is included in every Nethack distribution archive, but we wanted to call your attention to it here.

Generally, Nethack is freely available for distribution. You are encouraged to pass it on to friends, but you must pass a complete set of distribution files. You are not allowed to charge for copies, and you are not allowed to prevent others from sharing the game. Obviously, the purpose of the license is to make sure as many people as possible have a chance to get lost in the dungeons of doom!

Spoilers

Stuck? Desperate? Frustrated?

Go to the \CHAP02\NH-XTRAS\SPOILERS subdirectory. There are several files there that may prove invaluable.

The first is FAQ2.MAI. FAQ stands for Frequently Asked Questions. This particular FAQ is a "spoiler" FAQ; it's not very extensive, and for that reason, it's probably the best place to start. It'll give you just enough information to get you going without giving you so much that you'll feel intimidated.

SPOILERS.700 is a very large file written about Nethack 3.0. It represents quite a bit of work on the part of a very dedicated gaming team, and the information in it should help you survive and succeed. I suggest dipping into it only as you need to, however. Because it is so comprehensive, it can take away some of the fun of discovering things for yourself.

NETHAC.PS and NETHAC.DOC are for Nethack 3.1.0. (The information is still valid for release 3.1.3.) NETHAC.PS is not a readable file. It needs to be printed on a PostScript printer. If you have a PostScript printer connected to your machine, you can type **PRINT NETHAC.PS** and press (ENTER) or **COPY NETHACK.PS LPT1:** and press (ENTER). Either will work. NETHACK.PS is well organized, but incomplete. Some sections are not finished yet. (And it hasn't been spell-checked either, no pun intended.) Nevertheless, the material in here, especially about the new sections of Nethack 3.1.3, is invaluable. You will definitely need this information to understand the increased complexities of the dungeons. If you don't have a PostScript printer, then take a look at NETHAC.DOC. This is most of the same information, although not quite as well organized.

DATABASE is a file that has been extracted from the source code distribution for Nethack 3.1. It's a list of all of the monsters within the game. It's interesting reading because it gives you considerable background into the mythology of the creatures you will encounter in the dungeon.

ORACLES.TXT is a list of all of the pronouncements of the Oracle. With this file, you won't need to consult an oracle. You already know what she's going to say. This is a *very* valuable list of hints.

Two more files, RUMORS.FAL and RUMORS.TRU, list all of the hints you will find in fortune cookies. The first file contains those rumors that are false. The second lists those that are true. (I don't know how you feel about it, but I'm really annoyed at finding out the fortune cookies have been lying to me.)

Finally, BACKUP.EXE and RESTORE.EXE are cheat utilities to allow you unlimited reincarnations. The README.TXT file explains how to use them, but you don't really need these programs. You can accomplish the same result by copying your saved game to another directory. Nethack erases a saved game when you restore it, so if you get killed and need to resurrect yourself, you can copy your spare file back into the Nethack directory and you're ready to go again.

Happy Hacking!

Chrhack

by Mike Marcelais

Are you tired of looking at exclamation points and dollar signs. Wouldn't you much rather see little bottles and moneybags? Don't you think that monsters should look like monsters and not alphabet soup?

Chrhack is a nifty little add-on for Nethack 3.1 that changes the VGA font on your system, runs Nethack, and restores your system's normal fonts when you exit the game. This allows you to use alternate character sets for Nethack. You can even design your own characters for the game. CHREDIT.EXE, a font editor, is included.

Installation is fairly simple. First make a backup copy of NETHACK.CNF, in case you want to uninstall CHRHACK. Copy the CHRHACK files into the Nethack directory. Run INSTALL.EXE. Type **NH.BAT** to run Nethack instead of the usual Nethack command, and when the first dungeon map appears on your screen, the differences will be immediately obvious.

In the CHAP02\NH-XTRAS\CHRNEW subdirectory, you'll also find CHRNEW.ZIP, which contains an alternate character set to use with CHRHACK. Just copy it into the game directory. If you want to make up your own designs for Nethack's screens, use CHREDIT.EXE to generate your own CHRDATA.DAT file.

Directory:	\CHAP02\NH-XTRAS\CHRHACK	Contact:	Mike Marcelais
To Run:	**INSTALL.EXE, NH.BAT**		4109 Livingstone Place
Date:	1-31-93		Durham, NC 27707
Archive:	CHRHACK.ZIP		
	CHRNEW.ZIP		
Registration:	$10		

CHAPTER 3

PAC MAZES

PAC MAZES

Pac Man was the first true, video arcade game. A little yellow puck chomps his way through a maze, avoiding ghosts and eating energy pellets. Sometimes there's a cherry, a strawberry, or a banana to grab as well. Your goal is to see how much you can grab before you die. It's a metaphor for life.

Of course, Pac Man was an instant hit. And shortly after that, it became a worldwide phenomenon. Before the little yellow puck's popularity passed, he consumed billions, perhaps trillions of phosphor dots. At one point, Pac Man even had his own Saturday morning television show.

As a game, Pac Man had a slightly silly quality. The animation was simple, but its effectiveness was heightened by expressive sound effects. It required fast reflexes, hand-eye coordination, and an ability to think fast in a real-time situation. Many players learned the patterns of the game, so they could outwit the moving ghosts with monotonous regularity. At that level of involvement, Pac Man was no longer a game of speed, but a game of strategy.

Eventually Pac Man clones started showing up on desktop computers. By that time, the worst of the Pac Man craze had passed. Nevertheless, several of the games captured the charm of the original Pac Man and a few of them even surpassed it.

for Kids!

MAD MAZES

by Frederick Volking

Mad Mazes (Figure 3-1) is a very engrossing way to spend an hour or twelve. The program generates mazes at random, so you'll never see the same maze twice. There are ten levels here, each one harder than the last.

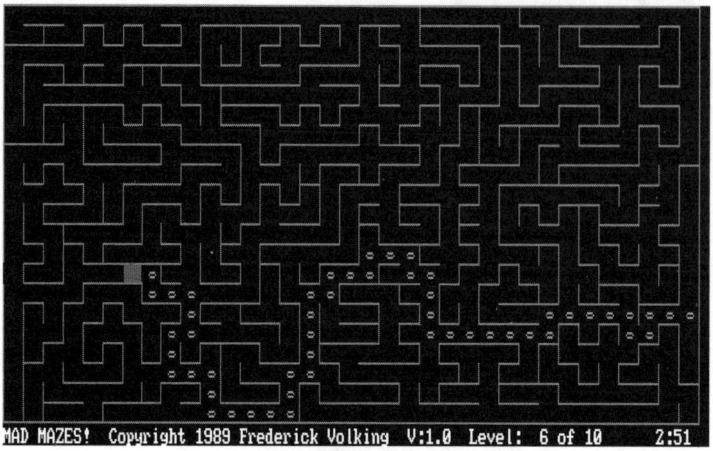

Figure 3-1
MAD MAZES
Keep playing. It gets a lot harder than this.

The mazes start out simple and become increasingly more complex. As the mazes grow more intricate, the lines on your screen get narrower. By the time you get to level 10, you'll be at the very limits of your computer monitor's resolution. The level 10 maze is *very* intimidating. Plan on spending a lot of time solving it.

In fact, the program will tell you exactly how long you took solving it. If you decide to give up, you can watch Mad Mazes solve the puzzle itself. Press (ESC) to do this. If you like mazes, like I do, this is a lot of fun.

Directory: \CHAP03\MADMAZES
To Play: **MMMMAZE.EXE**
Date: 8-30-89
Archive: MMMMAZE.ZIP
Registration: send a postcard

Contact: Frederick Volking
2335 Armada Way
San Mateo, CA 94404

for Kids!

PACMANIA

by Gregg Seelhoff

If you missed the Pac Man craze of the early eighties, Pacmania (Figure 3-2) captures most of the charm of the original game. It's also one of the most playable Pac Man clones we've seen.

Run, chew, chomp, chase, run, chew, chomp, chase, and so on. Just like real life.

Directory: \CHAP03\PACMANIA
To Play: **PACMANIA.EXE**
Date: 4-22-90
Archive: PACMANIA.ZIP
Registration: $10

Contact: Sophisticated Software Systems
P.O. Box 4936
East Lansing, MI 48826-4936

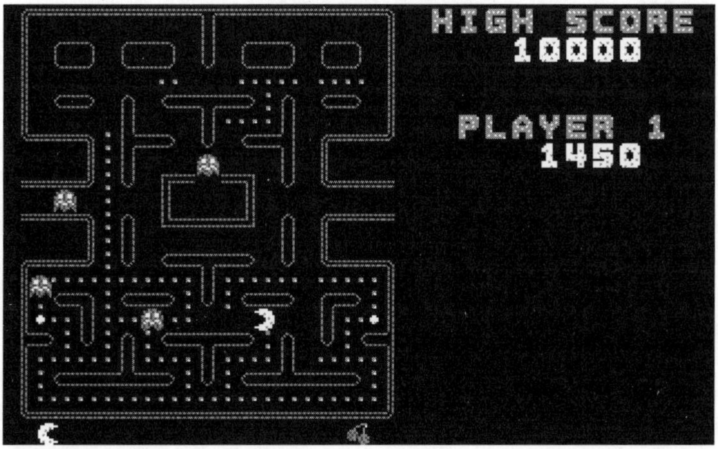

Figure 3-2
PACMANIA
Eat and run.

for Kids!

GOBMAN

by Filipe Mateus

Gobman is another Pac Man clone, but it is much more attractively implemented, and it has its own distinct personality. The mazes here are different. They're more colorful, and there are some nice surprises as you advance.

Unlike vanilla Pac Man, Gobman (Figure 3-3) gives you bombs to use against the ghosts. After you collect a bomb, you fire it by pressing the spacebar. If you run over an hourglass, you can halt all the ghosts for ten seconds. Sometimes there's a door that takes you directly to the next level, and there are even 1-ups to be caught that will give you an extra life. When you register, you get an upgrade with 50 new levels.

If classic Pac Man isn't challenging enough for you, try Gobman.

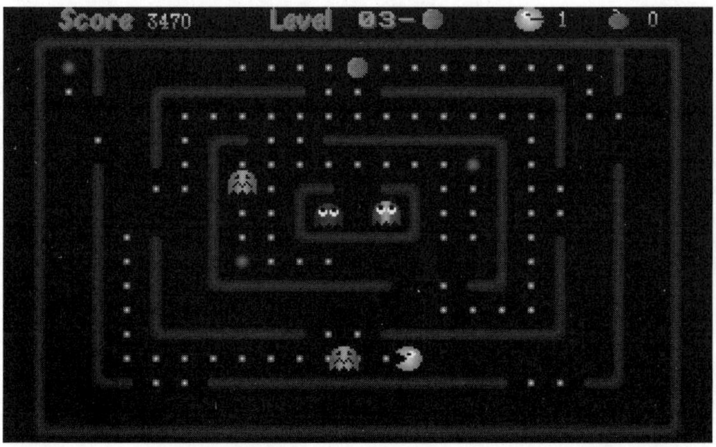

Figure 3-3
GOBMAN
You're still eating and running, but you're now in a better neighborhood.

Directory:	\CHAP03\GOBMAN	Contact:	Filipe Mateus
To Play:	**GOBMAN.EXE**		7128 Richard Hogen
Date:	4-22-90		St-Hubert, Quebec, Canada
Archive:	GOBMAN.ZIP		J3Y 8P6
Registration:	$13 (includes shipping)		

IMPEDE

by Louis DeSetto

for Kids!

Impede is one of my personal favorites. Not only because it's fun, but also because it's such a clear demonstration that the very best games are both elegant and simple.

Impede works like a cross between Pac Man and Centipede (see Figure 3-4). You have to navigate your way through a maze, eating dots. But every dot you eat adds one more link to your tail. Very shortly, half the maze is filled with your own length. If you bump into yourself, or if you can't continue, you lose.

Like the original Pac Man game, winning at Impede requires a different strategy for each maze. If you study some areas of the maze before you enter them, you'll see that they present serious problems of entry and exit, especially if you're dragging a long tail.

Impede looks easy, but you can spend a long time working your way through each level of this game. There are only six levels here, but that's more than enough to give you a full evening of challenges. The registered version gives you 30 more levels, and they're well worth it.

Directory:	\CHAP03\IMPEDE	Contact:	Louis DeSetto
To Play:	**IMPEDE.EXE**		118 Benjamin Street
Date:	8-9-93		Schenectady, NY 12303
Archive:	IMPEDE.ZIP		
Registration:	$12 (includes shipping)		

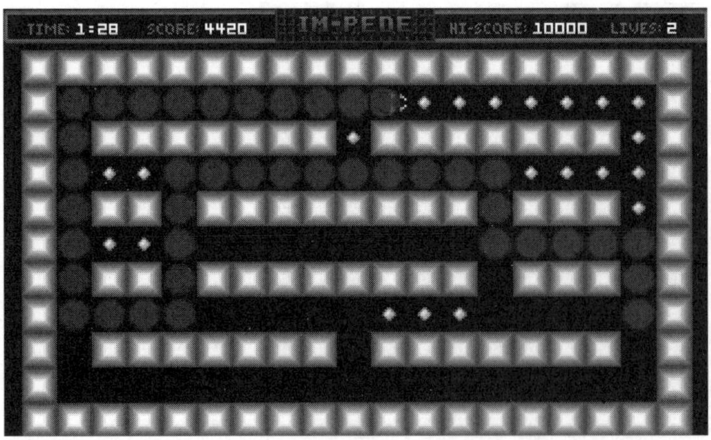

Figure 3-4
IMPEDE
Watch out for your tail. Unless your name is Ouroboros.

CHAPTER 4

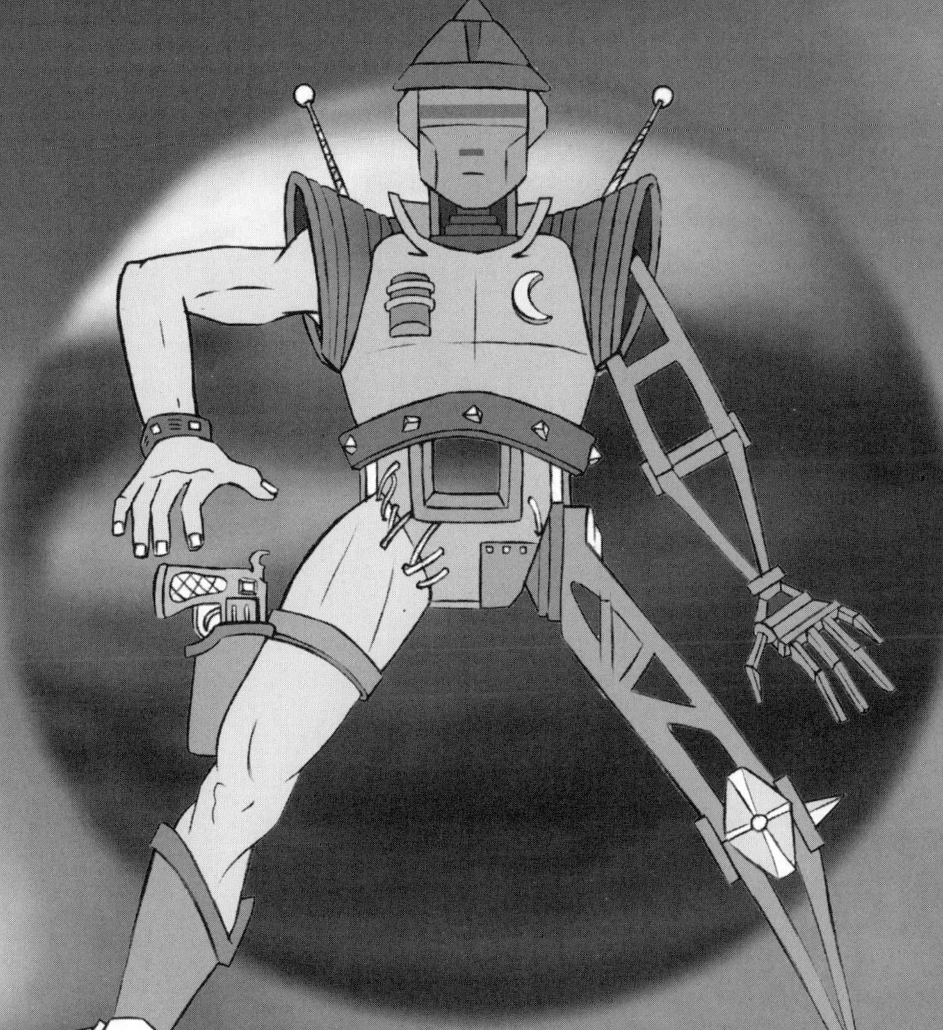

TETROIDS

TETROIDS

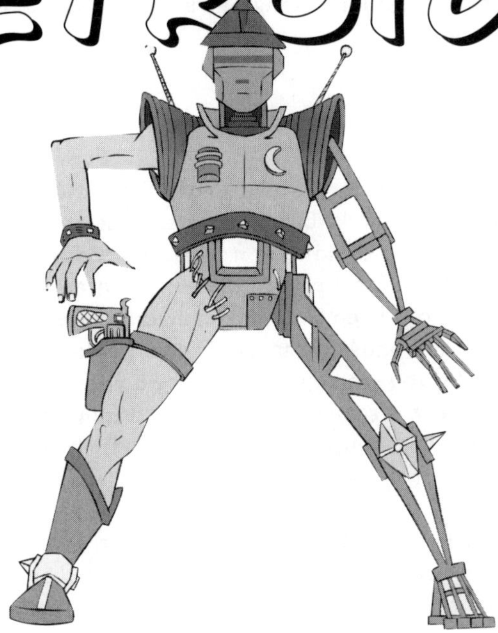

In 1987, Spectrum Holobyte introduced a new game to the United States. It was called Tetris. Created by two Soviet programmers, Tetris was both simple and elegant, and one of the great productivity destroyers of the eighties. It ate up time and processor cycles like few other games before it.

In case you've just arrived on this planet, Tetris is a kind of packing game. It's played in a vertical column. Colored pieces fall from the top of the screen, each one assembled from four square blocks. There are only seven possible shapes: left and right Ls, left and right doglegs, a square, a line, and a sort of triangle. Each piece is a different color. As the pieces fall, you can jockey them from one side of the column to the other. You may also rotate them. The object of the game is to fit the pieces together, leaving no spaces at all. Every time you complete a line, that line disappears. The game continues until the pieces pile up so high there's no room for any more to fall. The object of the game is to see how long you can keep going.

The game is intriguing to watch, and addicting to play. Ultimately, it's also maddening, because the more you play, the faster the pieces come dropping down. It's not possible to play Tetris *casually*. The game demands total involvement. You have to think ahead. You have to plan. You have to play as hard as you can.

Tetris was an immediate hit. No, it was more than a hit. It was a phenomenon. It was Pac Man all over again. It was a rare game of skill that held the attention of children, teens, and adults equally.

Of course, it didn't take long for Tetris clones to begin appearing as shareware. But the real excitement began when the programming community began to *improve* on the idea.

Here are several of the most interesting Tetris clones. You'll never look at a column of blocks the same way again.

for Kids!

ZENTRIS

by Robert J. Sundling

At first glance, Zentris (Figure 4-1) looks a little simple. Just clean attractive graphics and crisp Star Trek-like sounds. But if you press (ESC), you'll find a menu that gives you access to every feature you could want from a Tetris clone.

You can choose the look of the playing pieces, indented or solid; you can preview the next piece to fall; you can keep a running tally of your score; you can display how many of each piece has fallen; and you can even add a clock to the lower right corner of the screen – although why you would want to remind yourself of the time is something beyond comprehension. *Serious* gamers don't pay any attention to clocks.

Zentris can be played with mouse, keyboard, or joystick. It's handsome, it's responsive, and it pretty much lives up to its billing as "the best 'Tris in the world." Certainly it's the best we've seen.

Zentris comes with a 14-page ZENTRIS.DOC file. Registered users receive a copy of the game that has some features not implemented in the shareware version. The bad news is that Zentris is *every bit as addicting* as the original Tetris.

Directory:	\CHAP04\ZENTRIS
To Play:	**ZENTRIS.EXE**
Date:	8-3-92
Archive:	ZENTRIS.ZIP
Registration:	$10

Contact: Robert J. Sundling
ZenSoft
200 Rowe Street
Stoughton, WI 53589-2352
BBS: Bob Sundling at Synergy BBS
Tel: 608-277-0280
Fidonet: Bob Sundling at NineJackNine
1:121/99

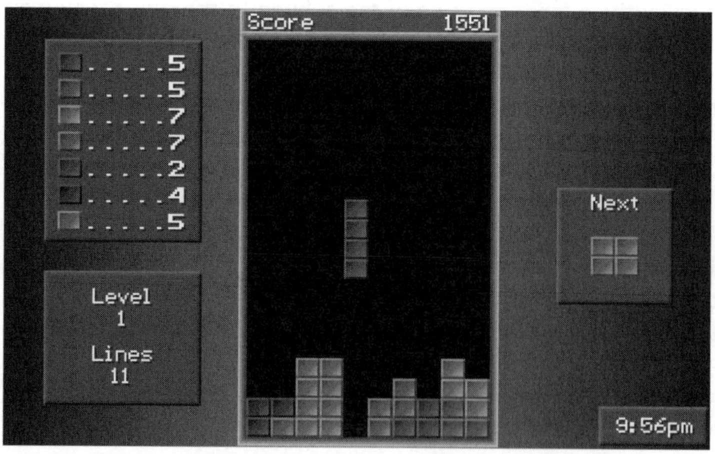

Figure 4-1
ZENTRIS
A classic game in a handsome implementation.

for Kids!

ROTAKTIX

by Loyd L. Tove

Rotaktix is a different kind of tetroid. Here, you get to drop a whole row of blocks at a time. Wherever you get three or more lined up vertically, horizontally, or diagonally, they disappear, and the blocks above them drop down. This can produce additional combinations of disappearing blocks, so it's possible with one lucky move to trigger a cascade, or even an avalanche.

As you can see in Figure 4-2, the game field has nine wells, each of which will hold seven blocks. When a row of blocks appears across the top of the screen, you slide them right or left to line them up above the desired wells. Pressing the SPACE BAR drops them in the well. Keep in mind that you have a limited amount of time to decide where to drop the blocks; when time runs out, the blocks drop automatically.

The game is played in rounds; first you have to eliminate fifteen rows horizontally, then fifteen rows vertically, then fifteen diagonally; then you get a bonus round. Then it gets tougher; a new color gets added to the mix, so it gets even more difficult to match up three or more blocks of the same kind. Thank goodness for the wild cards that match any adjacent tokens.

Actually, the best way to learn this game is boot it up and play it. You'll understand how it works in far less time than it takes to read this explanation.

Directory: CHAP04/ROTAKTIX
To Play: **ROTAKTIX.EXE**
Date: 12-05-93
Archive: ROTAK0.ZIP
Registration: $19

Contact: Data Wave Software
13500 SW Pacific Highway #457
Portland, OR 97223

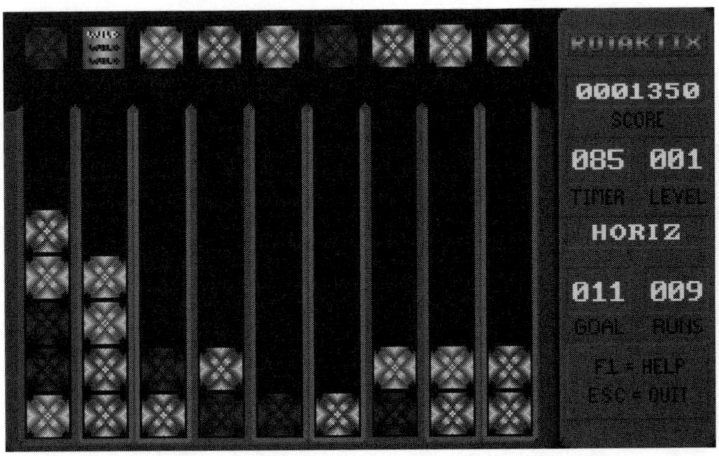

Figure 4-2
ROTAKTIX
The combination of strategy, color, and sound will dazzle and delight you.

QUATRIS II PLUS

by Eugene Kim and Hong Kim

Quatris II Plus is an elegantly crafted elaboration on the original Tetris game. It has an interesting history behind it, too.

Eugene Kim wrote the first Quatris when he was 16 years old for a high school programming contest; the program won first place. Quatris was followed by Quatris Pro, then the author wrote Quatris II Plus at the age of 19, while studying at UC Berkeley. His brother Hong added some features.

Like the original Tetris, you have to guide falling blocks into place to fill lines at the bottom of the screen. Unlike the original Tetris, this game doesn't go on until you drop from exhaustion. It's played in rounds, where you win by completing a certain number of rows per round.

The big difference in this implementation (see Figure 4-3) is that the width of the playing field will vary from one round to the next, and the block shapes are different than you've seen anywhere else. In addition to the standard set of quadruple blocks, there are sets of single blocks, double blocks, triple blocks, and more. You will also be bombarded by sets of unconnected blocks as well. These can be especially challenging.

Besides the new shapes, there are bombs you can detonate to wipe shapes off the screen; but the penalty for using a bomb is that it reduces your score and your energy; some bombs even increase the number of rows you need to destroy to win the round!

In addition to all this, there's a bonus game played between rounds, a memory game which awards you extra points and energy. The game isn't too hard to learn, but mastering its intricacies may take some time. Fortunately, you may save your game and resume it later, after you've had a chance to lie down and rest for a while.

Directory: \CHAP04\QUATRIS
To Play: **Q2PLUS.EXE**
Date: 02-09-94
Archive: QUATRIS.ZIP
Registration: $20

Contact: Awesome Softworx, Inc.
4157 West 5th Street, Suite 222
Los Angeles, CA 90020
BBS: 818-701-7465

Figure 4-3
QUATRIS II PLUS
The varied playing fields and unusual shapes make this tetroid variant quite challenging

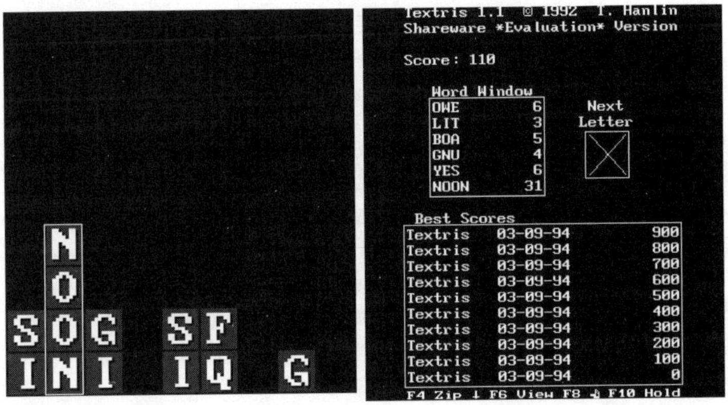

Figure 4-4
TEXTRIS
Can you spell Textris? I knew you could.

for Kids!

TEXTRIS

by Thomas G. Hanlin

Textris (Figure 4-4) is a combination of Tetris and Scrabble. Letters drop one at a time from the top of the screen. You maneuver them into place with the intention of forming them into 3-letter, 4-letter, and 5-letter words. Whenever you form a word, either horizontally or vertically, the word is outlined and then the letters blink out. Any letters still above will drop down to fill the empty spaces; as in Beyond Columns, this can trigger a cascade of disappearing blocks.

Occasionally a blank drops down from the top of the screen. You can assign it a letter value before it touches down. If you don't, then a random letter will be selected for you.

Like Tetris, the goal of the game is to see how long you can play before the playing field fills up. The game probably has some educational value, but that's the wrong reason for anyone to play it. This is one you play for fun.

The dictionary for this game contains 90,000 words. Including "KAT." The registered version of Textris comes with a dictionary editor, so you can put in "DAWG," I guess.

Directory: \CHAP04\TEXTRIS
To Play: **TEXTRIS.EXE**
Date: 11-25-92
Archive: TEXTRIS.ZIP
Registration: $11.95

Contact: Thomas G. Hanlin III
3544 E. Southern Ave. #104
Mesa, AZ 85204

NYET3: REVENGE OF THE MUTANT STONES

by Peter Schnitzer, Stephan Goth, Ralf Mohmeyer, and Michael Kriegel

I started playing NYET3 (shown in Figure 4-5), not knowing what to expect. At first, I thought it was just another tetroid — it was attractive enough, the graphics were crisp, it had clever sound effects and music, and even a Monty Python-like figure on the opening screens.

But then . . . as one of my carefully targeted pieces came dropping down, part of the piece beneath it *crumbled* away, leaving me with a gaping hole that I couldn't fill. As annoying as that was, I couldn't help it, I started laughing. Here was a game written by a practical joker! When you lose, the game even screams in agony. This is Tetris with a vengeance — literally.

Actually, it's not just one game; it's *many* games in one, each one a game of discovery as well as skill. As with Sretriss, you have to tackle successive challenges. Each one is different, and every one you beat, gives you the opportunity to take on the next. Here, the goal is not to survive as long as you can, but to survive the falls of a set number of pieces. If you can do that, you win the round.

The more challenges you complete, the more "money" you have in the game bank. Before you begin the next round, you can go to the "store" and buy "weapons" to use, tools that you can apply to help clear a line of blocks. As you progress, the game play becomes ever more elaborate. This is not a game to be played *casually*.

My only complaint about the game is that you have to press the arrow key for each sideways move you want to make. Holding it down does not produce a repeat-key function. This is the only flaw in an otherwise fine game, and it's a minor one; very quickly, you will adapt your style of play. Nevertheless, it will give you a moment's pause the first time, so be aware of that.

NYET3 comes from a team of talented German authors, and it demonstrates the ever-changing personality of tetroid games. The shareware version has only 36 levels and 6 special tasks. After you master it, you can order the registered version with 126 levels and 21 special tasks. You didn't really need to have a life, did you?

Directory: \CHAP04\NYET3
To Play: **START.BAT**
Date: 7-6-93
Archive: NYET3.ZIP
Registration: $35 + $5 shipping

Contact: Pearl America Inc.
41281/2 California Ave SW
Seattle, WA 98116
Tel: 206-938-0336
Fax: 206-938-0338
CIS: 71043, 674

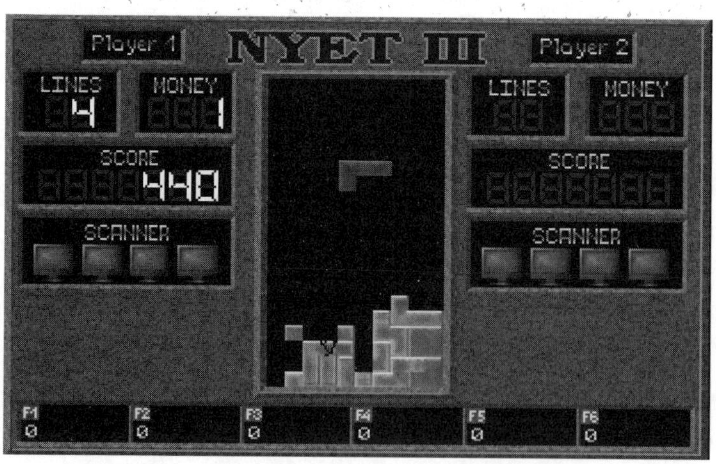

Figure 4-5
NYET3
Watch for crumbling stones.

SQUAREZ

by Adam Pederson

Squarez (Figure 4-6) is a different kind of Tetris clone. It isn't played in a column, it's played on a square field. You have to maneuver pieces into place to form rectangular blocks. Whenever you form a rectangle, it disappears, but it leaves behind the fragments of connecting blocks, which remain in your way when you try to place the next piece.

You can play Squarez as an ordinary packing game; you can play the "normal" game, which includes a selection of special tiles, or you can play the chaotic extreme mode, in which you can never be too sure what will happen when you place a piece. Special tiles include hazardous chemicals, devastator bombs, and destructive missiles. And of course, there's always the *splooge* to watch out for.

Squarez lets you play against the clock, or against another player in real time. (If you're using the keyboard, don't expect the ↑ to turn the pieces. Use CONTROL and ALT to rotate the blocks.)

However you approach it, you're going to find that Squarez is a seductive toy. Its graphics and sound effects are delicious, and the challenge of its puzzles will keep you playing much longer than you thought you were going to.

Highly recommended for those who have too much spare time.

Directory:	\CHAP04\SQUAREZ
To Play:	**SQUAREZ.EXE**
Date:	7-31-93
Archive:	SQUAREZ.ZIP
Registration:	$22 (includes shipping)

Contact: Software Creations
26 Harris St.
Clinton, MA 01510
Orders: 508-368-8654
Fax: 508-365-7214

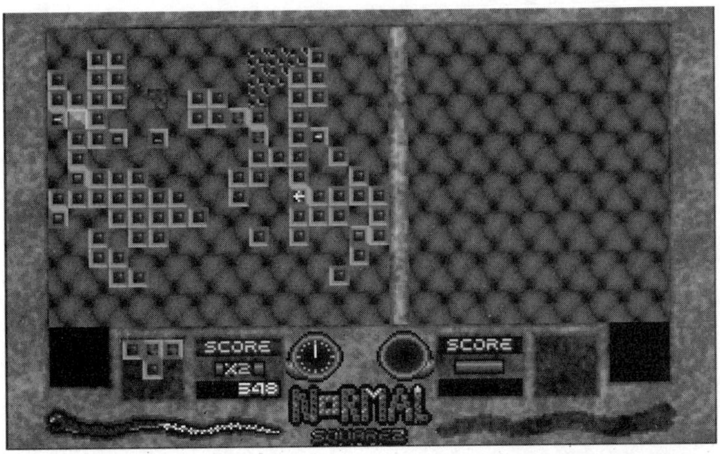

Figure 4-6
SQUAREZ
This is the normal mode. Beware of chaos.

CHAPTER 5

'NOIDS

'NOIDS

For a short while at the end of the eighties, it seemed as though every video arcade in America was dominated by a game called Arkanoids, an expansion of an earlier game called Breakout. It was a kind of one-player Ping-Pong.

In a Breakout-type game, you have a wall of bricks, a ball, and a paddle. Every time the ball bounces off a brick, the brick disappears. Sometimes it drops a bonus down that you have to catch — or a bomb that you have to avoid. Bonuses can provide all sorts of advantages: they can slow down the ball, make it super-destructive, double the size of the paddle, or give you an extra life. Bombs, on the other hand, can speed up the ball, make it invisible, or just blow up your paddle when they hit it. You have to figure out which colors of falling bricks to catch and which colors to avoid.

As with Tetris, clone versions of Arkanoids began showing up very quickly. The game is deceptively simple. It looks much easier to play than it really is; it requires great hand-eye coordination, visual acuity, and quick reflexes. It only *looks* mindless. In truth, it requires a player to be totally involved. In many ways, 'noids are the definitive arcade games.

We found three that we thought were particularly well crafted.

TUROID

by Jason Truong

Turoid (Figure 5-1) is a very addictive game. And that's an understatement. This was built with a great deal of thought, meaning some very nasty tricks await you. You'll find out once you start playing. Like other paddle-ball games, you're going to need fast reflexes, but this is a game of strategy and tactics too.

The left mouse button shoots the ball left; the right button shoots it right. The ball either bounces off a brick or shatters it, depending on the brick's color. Green shatters immediately, orange after two hits, white after three. Yellow bricks can only be destroyed by power or super balls. You complete the level when all of the green, orange, and white bricks are destroyed.

The real challenge lies in the purple and gold bricks. These drop large purple and gold balls on you. Avoid the purple balls; grab the gold ones. Purple brings you bad luck. Sometimes the ceiling opens and purple balls drop on you for no reason at all, just because you're there.

Fortunately, the gold balls bring good luck, including wider paddles, extra paddles (very rare), extra balls, shooting laser paddles, sticky paddles which let you catch the ball and hold it, and sometimes even slow down all the balls on the screen. But remember, the only falling object that you want to catch is the gold ball.

A slowdown utility will probably be useful for those over 13.

Directory:	\CHAP05\TUROID
To Play:	**TUROID.EXE**
Date:	01-17-94
Archive:	TUROID.ZIP
Registration:	$10

Contact: Jason Truong
12167 Achilles Street
Norwalk, CA 90650-1824

Figure 5-1
TUROID
Not just another brick in the wall.

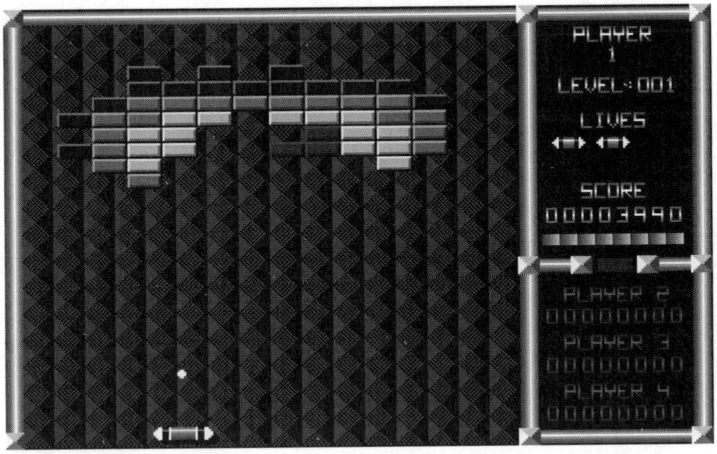

Figure 5-2
AQUANOID
Tear down the wall!

AQUANOID

by Stefan Heineke and Karsten Finger

Aquanoid (Figure 5-2) is another handsome effort out of Germany. There are a great many talented programmers in Europe and we're starting to see some of their best efforts.

Aquanoid is more configurable than Bananoid. The shareware version allows one- or two-player games. (The registered version allows up to four players.) You can also configure mouse and game speed, but as with many of the arcade games in this collection, if you're running a fast machine, you might need a slowdown utility.

The bad news is that most of the documentation files traveling with Aquanoid are in German. The good news is that you probably won't need to read them.

Directory: \CHAP05\AQUANOID
To Play: **START.BAT**
Date: 1-31-93
Archive: AQUANOID.ZIP
Registration: $20

Contact: Stefan Heineke
Anton-G.-Str. 36
2942 Jever
Germany

BIPBOP2

by D. Stuart Riffle

Your objective in BIPBOP (Figure 5-3) is to remove all "boinks" from the screen. A boink is a little box with a Roman numeral in it. Whenever you bounce your ball against a boink, its value decreases. Knock a boink down to zero and it disappears. When all of the boinks on a level are destroyed, you advance to the next level. There are twenty in all.

As with other 'noid games, you use the mouse to control the paddle, but there's an interesting addition. If you press either mouse button, the paddle fires a missile which

Figure 5-3
BIPBOP2
Can you bip the boinks?

has the power to deflect the ball. This can be very useful for keeping the ball on one side of the screen or the other. Or, if the ball gets trapped bouncing between two corners, you can break it free with a well-placed shot.

And yes, you're probably going to find a slowdown utility helpful here. The game is machine-sensitive, and even at its slowest speed, it's still too fast on newer machines.

The documentation for BipBop2 is almost as much fun as the game. The author has obviously been seduced by the Silly Side of the Force.

Directory: \CHAP05\BIPBOP2
To Play: **BIPBOP2.EXE**
Date: 4-27-92
Archive: BIPBOP2.ZIP
Registration: $20

Contact: S&M Software
2320 Brimhall Court, Suite 101
Deltona, FL 32738-8747
Attn: BipBop II

CHAPTER 6

PUZZLES

PUZZLES

Remember the erstwhile computer expert who said that there are really only six kinds of computer games? Well, if that's true, then all adventure games are really just variations on Pac Man and all computer puzzles are just variants on Solitaire. All you're doing is rearranging pieces on a playing field.

What's amazing is that there are so *many* different ways to do it.

Most computer puzzles exist as a combination of art and challenge. They are pretty to look at and they're fun to play with. Puzzles also have the unique property of exercising that part of our mind that we need to exercise the most, the *problem-solving* part. It's my firm belief that playing with puzzles makes us smarter in the same way that going to the gym and working out on the exercise machines makes us stronger.

We found a fascinating set of puzzles for you to play with. Yes, they look good on your monitor, but they also present a series of seductive challenges that you can come back to again and again and again.

HEXIPUZZLES

by Preston Frey

Hexipuzzles (seen in Figure 6-1) is an attractive solitaire game. Your job is to place multicolored triangles in the playing field so that the colored sides match up like dominoes. There are 40 different playing fields to fill and two levels of difficulty. If this isn't enough, you can design your own screens too.

Both my son Dennis and I found Hexipuzzles an enjoyable diversion, not so much a puzzle as an interesting pastime. It doesn't seem as obsessive as some puzzles; you can

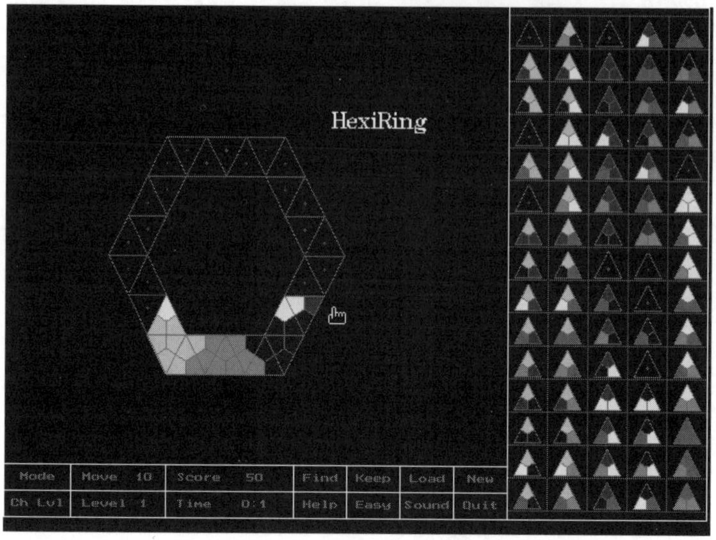

Figure 6-1
HEXIPUZZLES

quit in the middle without feeling you're betraying something. I like it because it's the perfect solitaire game for when you're on the telephone and someone puts you on hold.

Directory:	\CHAP06\HEXIPUZ	Contact:	Preston Frey
To Play:	**HEXIPUZ3.EXE**		306 W. Wahalla Lane
Date:	8-8-93		Phoenix, AZ 85027-4417
Archive:	HEXIPUZ.ZIP		Tel: 602-516-1250
Registration:	$10 (for solutions and source code)		

GAMES MAGAZINE® PRESENTS WORD PUZZLES

programming by Michael Hausman
puzzle development and selection, and documentation by Lou Kesten
program graphics by Gabi Ladowski
music by Dan Froehlich, David Bredesen

Games Magazine Presents Word Puzzles (the main menu is shown in Figure 6-2) is a sophisticated, feature-packed collection of the kind of logic games you're used to seeing in Sunday's paper.

You'll find: crossword puzzles, cryptograms (coded messages which you solve by substituting one letter for another), double crosses (answer clues to complete a message), quote boxes (unscramble mixed letters to get a celebrity's statement), and word scrambles (use provided letters to spell out words associated with a selected subject).

This is a truly elegant, enjoyable implementation of a familiar variety of games. When you first start, you can sign in by pressing TAB or double clicking on the "LOG ON" button in the upper left of the main menu screen. Select a type of game by either click-

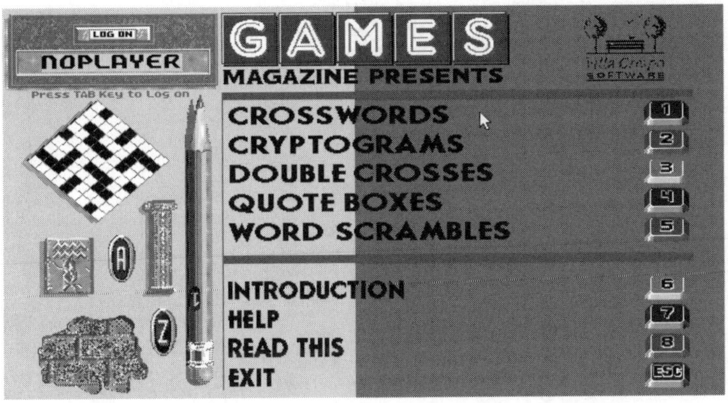

Figure 6-2
Games Magazine Presents WORD PUZZLES, a potpourri of wordy challenges.

ing on the games with the mouse or pressing 1 through 5. Each game includes its own set of instructions, which you can view by pressing F10.

When playing, pressing F5 gives a hint; pressing twice solves the whole puzzle. We did notice that while loading games, the screen tended to flicker somewhat, but this doesn't take anything away from this entertaining package.

Directory: \CHAP06\WORDPUZL
To Play: **GAMES.BAT (VGA)**
GAMES16.BAT (SVGA)
Date: 5-18-94
Archive: WRDPUZ.ZIP
Registration: $29.95 + shipping and handling

Contact: MVP Software
1035 Dallas SE
Grand Rapids, MI 49507-8376
U.S. and Canadian orders: 800-968-9684
Other orders: 616-245-8376
Fax: 616-245-3204

BLOCK-MAN

by Doug and Larry Murk

Long ago, in the kingdom of Bentangle, King Triangulous sought a clever husband for his daughter Princess Pentagwin. He designed 17 rooms and carefully placed blocks in each of them, creating a series of devious obstacle courses. Only a worthwhile suitor would be clever enough to cross the rooms.

You, as love-struck Block-Man (shown in Figure 6-3), have accepted the King's challenge to claim the princess' hand. In order to pass through a room, you have to maneuver and use the blocks correctly. You'll have to pick up boxes and move them so you can climb over walls. Sometimes you bring a box over the wall, so you can scale the next barrier. It's all about moving boxes around and stacking them so you can get to more boxes so you can move them around and stack them too. (This game is the kind of practice you need if you're thinking about moving.)

The left, right, and up arrow keys move Block-Man, and the down arrow key lets him pick up or drop blocks. He picks up and drops in the direction he's facing. You can also undo moves (press U) or get help (press ?). After you solve each problem, your rating is displayed on an IQ chart, and you can take a crack at a harder problem.

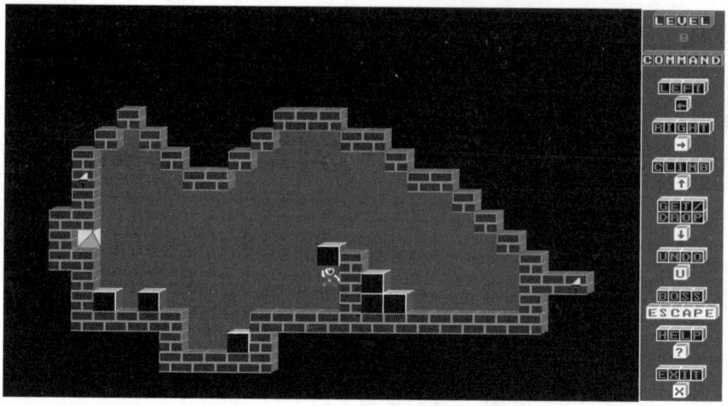

Figure 6-3:
BLOCKMAN
Get me outta here!

Some users might find the interface a little clumsy, since the game is designed for EGA, but the challenges here are creative, and it's well worth a look.

Directory:	\CHAP06\BLOCKMAN
To Play:	**BMAN1.EXE**
Date:	08-01-93
Archive:	BLOCKMAN.ZIP
Registration:	$14

Contact: Soleau Software
163 Amsterdam Avenue, Suite 213
New York, NY 10023
Tel: 212-721-2361
Fax: 212-873-4994

SHERLOCK

by Everett Kaser

Here's a totally unique computer game. There is nothing else like this program anywhere. It's one of a kind. Be warned, however. Sherlock is addictive. It's easy to learn and it can keep you hooked for hours, days, weeks, and even months. I have friends I haven't heard from since I gave them this game. So don't get into this if your family is going to need you soon. (Like any time this year.)

What is Sherlock? It's a game of deduction. (See Figure 6-4.)

Remember those really frustrating logic puzzles? You know the ones. Mr. Jones lives next door to the man who owns the brown car. The bald man lives in the white house. Mr. Smith is allergic to cats. Mr. White is a veterinarian. Who drives the Mustang? You had to draw a chart just to figure out who was who.

Sherlock is the computer version. The relationships here are all graphical. There are six columns, you have to deduce which face belongs with which house, which number, which letter, which fruit, and which street sign. There are two types of clues, vertical and horizontal. The vertical clues are along the bottom of the screen. If baby-face is over the white house, for instance, that tells you that baby-face and the white house are in the same column.

The horizontal clues are a little trickier. If baldy (aka Picard) is between two strawberries, that tells you that he is next to the column with the strawberry. So if you know

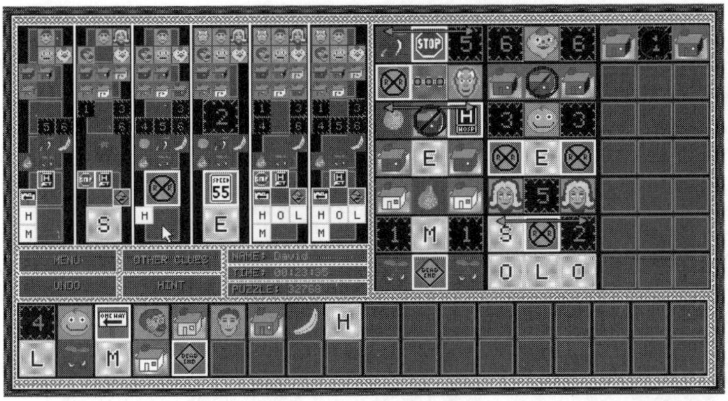

Figure 6-4
SHERLOCK
I think Colonel Mustard did it in the Conservatory with Miss Scarlet.

that the strawberry has to be in the same column with the stop sign, then Picard can only be in one of the columns on either side. There are also clues that tell you that two elements are *not* next to each other, or that one is to the left of another, or that one item is between two other items.

The game is extremely well designed. There are 65,536 different combinations of elements, so there's no shortage of puzzles to solve, and there's even a hint button to help you if you get stuck. Sherlock also keeps track of different players' progress through the puzzle combinations. So if you're working on puzzle 9,087 and your friend is working on puzzle 3,294, the program will remember that and return you each to the appropriate puzzle number. There's even a built-in timer if you want to play tournament mode.

If you don't like the default set of image tiles in this game, you can load an alternate set; several are provided in the directory \CHAP06\SHERLOCK\NEWTILES. If you don't like any of the alternate image tiles, the program has a built-in drawing tool for designing your own. What more could you ask for? I wish all computer games were as thoughtfully designed and presented as Sherlock.

Directory:	\CHAP06\SHERLOCK
To Play:	**SHERLOCK.EXE**
Date:	7-6-94
Archive:	SHERLOCK.ZIP
Registration:	$15

Contact: Everett Kaser
Sherlock
35405 Spruce St.
Albany, OR 97321
Tel: 503-928-5259
Weekdays: 6:00pm - 9:00pm PST
Weekends: 8:30am - 9:00pm PST
CompuServe: 70673,1547

We have included several additional files of alternate image tiles for Sherlock. Any file with an .SHI extension is an alternate image set, which you can load from Sherlock's menu. (Be sure to check out the subdirectories in \SHERLOCK\NEWTILES; you'll find the sets archived there.) All are fun to look at. I suspect, however, that you may find some of the files more appropriate for actual game play than others. Have fun!

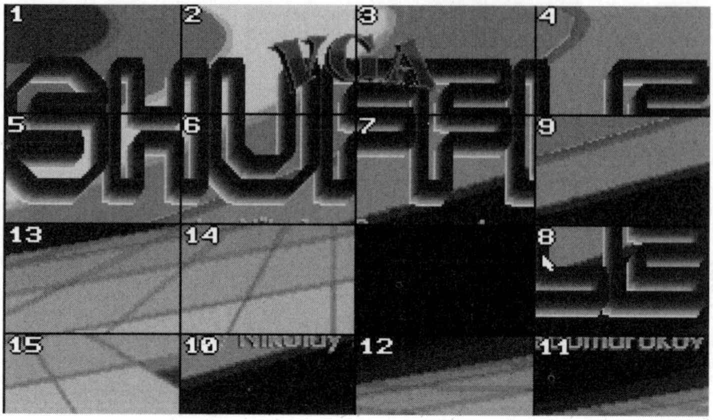

Figure 6-5
SHUFFLE
A classic puzzle with a new face.

for Kids!

SHUFFLE

by Nikolai Soumarokov

When I was a child, I was given a "15" puzzle. It kept me quiet for hours. (I have no doubt that my parents did it deliberately. I have the same thought in mind when I buy toys for Dennis.) The "15" puzzle was a small box with 15 numbered tiles that could be slid horizontally and vertically. The idea was to put the tiles in numerical order. Shuffle is the same puzzle, only updated to use graphic images instead of numbered tiles.

Shuffle (Figure 6-5), however, is an enhanced version of "15." In Shuffle, you are able to choose the size of the playing field. It can be 4x4, 5x5, 6x6… all the way up to 10x10. The largest size gives you 99 separate tiles to unscramble.

It's very easy to move the pieces in this game. Simply left-click on the piece you want to slide into the blank space. That's it. A right-click brings up the game menu.

Working with pictures can be confusing sometimes, so Shuffle allows you to view the assembled picture at any time. This is a valuable hint function when you're playing some of the larger fields.

Shuffle comes with three pictures, but you can add your own if you want. It's a great game for introducing young children to the computer, especially if you install their own picture or a picture of the family dog or cat into the puzzle. (You'll need to convert your picture to the appropriate image format to do this, however. See the documentation.)

Directory: \CHAP06\SHUFFLE
To Play: **SHUFFLE.EXE**
Date: 12-9-91
Archive: SHUFFLE.ZIP
Registration: $0

Contact: Nikolai Soumarokov
Zschokkegasse 91/2/5/25
1220 Vienna, Austria

CHAPTER 7

PACKING

PACKING

Packing puzzles are all about position. Can you maneuver the boxes out of the way to get to the reward? A packing puzzle *always* looks easier than it really is. You take one look and you think you see an obvious answer. Sure. Just push this here and that there. And then suddenly you discover that you've boxed yourself in. A well-designed packing puzzle can have the intricacy of a chess problem.

Generally, packing-type puzzles present you with a playing field filled with various kinds of objects. You have to rearrange the objects, pushing them out of the way, so you can get to the treasures or the exit.

Looked at one way, this is another variant on adventure: you have to get past the obstacles to get to the goodies. But it's also a maze game, because you often have to navigate through precarious channels. And it's *also* a kind of solitaire, because you're rearranging pieces to produce a result. Once again the distinctions start to blur.

Never mind all that. A game is not a theory, it's a challenge. Here are several of our favorites.

SOKOBAN
by Jim Radcliffe

The Japanese word *sokoban* means "warehouse man." A Sokoban puzzle is one in which you have to push boxes around a playing field to get them into a designated position. The key word is "push." That's the only way you can move anything. You have to push it to its destination. You can't pull.

Figure 7-1
SOKOBAN
Beautiful and challenging. Can you keep yourself from getting boxed in?

This means that if you push a box up against a wall, or up against another box, you can't get behind it to push it away again. So you have to be careful not to push a box into a corner, and you have to make sure that you don't accidentally create a pile of boxes that you can't move. Four boxes in a square can be a nasty mistake.

While most Sokoban-type games force you to solve each challenge in turn, Sokoban allows you to select your challenges by name. Some are easier than others. In fact, some are dang near impossible. Sokoban also comes with an editor so you can generate your own puzzles, but only the registered version lets you save your puzzles to disk. The registered version also comes with more puzzles to tax your ingenuity.

Jim Radcliffe wrote this version of Sokoban (Figure 7-1) because so many people who registered his Sokoball game (see the following section) also wanted a standard Sokoban game, but with the same elegant and graceful graphics. The puzzles here were not created by Radcliffe; he wrote the code for the game, but not the puzzles themselves. The puzzles are the creation of Hans de Vreught of the Netherlands and others who contributed. All are public domain. All of them are (allegedly) solvable.

Have fun. Sokoban is a classic.

Directory:	\CHAP07\SOKOBAN	Contact:	Jim Radcliffe
To Play:	**SOKO94SW.EXE**		P.O. Box 823
Date:	1-1-94		Coppell, TX 75019
Archive:	SOKO94SW.ZIP	CompuServe E-mail to:	
Registration:	$10		Jim Radcliffe
			72307,3077

for Kids!

SOKOBALL

by Jim Radcliffe

Sokoball (See Figure 7-2) is Jim Radcliffe's expansion of the Sokoban idea. You still use the big yellow ball to "push" the boxes. Unfortunately, now the playing field is littered with some very unorthodox traps. There are holes to fall into, arrows that will kick you off sideways, pop-up barriers, one-way streets, and floor plans that change when you cross specific tiles.

Like Sokoban, Sokoball allows you to select your challenges by name. Some are easier than others. In fact, some look to be impossible, and will require considerable work.

Sokoball also comes with an editor so you can generate your own puzzles, but most of the neat features of the editor are in the the registered version. (Read SOKOBALL.DOC for more information.) Unfortunately, there is no guarantee with either game editor that you won't invent an impossible puzzle, so be careful.

As with Sokoban, this is one of the most beautiful packing games we've seen anywhere.

Directory:	\CHAP07\SOKOBALL
To Play:	**SOKOBALL.EXE**
Date:	8-26-93
Archive:	SOKOBALL.ZIP
Registration:	$10

Contact: Jim Radcliffe
P.O. Box 823
Coppell, TX 75019
CompuServe E-mail to:
Jim Radcliffe
72307,3077

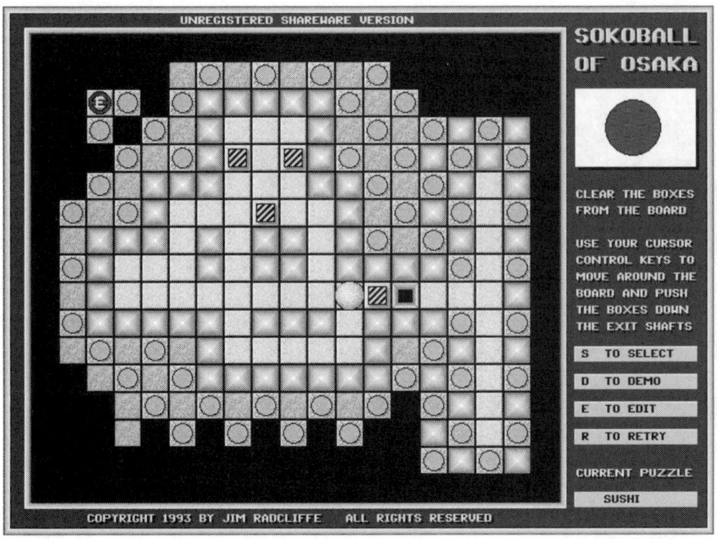

Figure 7-2
SOKOBALL
Sokoban with traps. Not for the unwary.

PAGANITZU

by Keith Schuler

for Kids!

Paganitzu (shown in Figure 7-3) holds a special place in my heart. It was the first shareware game I ever registered. I started playing around with it one lazy afternoon. I had no expectations; I thought the game was harmless, merely a diversion . . . until my son wandered in three hours later and asked me if I was ever going to fix dinner. The next day, I sent a check to Apogee.

Paga (for short) is a packing game with some arcade elements. If you don't have the reflexes for another scrolling-action, ledge-jumping, arcade-style, shoot-em-up adventure, you'll find Paganitzu a refreshing alternative. It's a game of logic and forethought where planning is more important than speed.

You are Alabama Jones, and your job is to explore an ancient Aztec pyramid. As you go deeper and deeper into the ruin, you are presented with a series of challenges. Each challenge consists of one or more rooms containing both diamonds and boulders. You have to push the boulders aside to get to the diamonds, but you have to be careful not to push the boulders into impassable piles, or you won't be able to get all the diamonds or get to the exit. As with all packing games, it's a matter of careful positioning.

New elements are introduced with each puzzle: venom-spitting snakes; pools of water into which you can push boulders; giant, red, man-eating spiders; breakable walls; crossbows; traps; and so on. Each puzzle teaches you another interaction of the elements, so as you proceed, the adventure becomes progressively more difficult. Some of the screens may keep you challenged for hours.

Although Paganitzu is not an arcade-action game, there are one or two screens where you will need to outrun the giant red spiders. Unfortunately, the game is speed-sensitive, so if you're running this on a fast 486 machine, or better, you'll need to install a slowdown utility first. For most of this game, however, you aren't going to need quick

Figure 7-3
PAGANITZU
A clever mix of adventure game and packing puzzle.

reflexes, only a quick mind. The majority of the puzzles are static; nothing happens unless you trigger it by your move.

Paganitzu only looks simple. That's a large part of its charm; each puzzle *seems* so easy, but be prepared to get hooked. Once you start, you won't rest until you've completed the entire quest, and that *will* take awhile. Set an alarm so you won't forget to feed your kids.

Directory:	\CHAP07\PAGANITZ
To Play:	**PAGA1.EXE**
Date:	12-1-91
Archive:	PAGA1.ZIP
BBS Archive:	\CHAP07\PAGANITZ\BBS
Registration:	$35 (for all three episodes, includes shipping)

Contact: Apogee Software
P.O. Box 496389
Garland, TX 75049
Tel: 800-GAME-123

CRATES

by Mark Batchelor

Crates, shown in Figure 7-4, is a classic packing game. You are a warehouseman who has to push a bunch of boxes into their proper places; you've got to slide them on the squares marked with diamonds. Each time you get the place organized, you're given a harder mess to straighten up.

Use the arrow keys to direct the warehouseman. The down arrow key lets you pick up or put down boxes in the direction you are facing. Remember to try to avoid pushing a crate against a perimeter wall, unless you can push it into place; that's the surest way to get yourself stuck.

The game doesn't display better than EGA resolution, so the graphics aren't as lush as what you might expect from recently designed efforts. The shareware version doesn't include all the bells and whistles, either; particularly challenging (frustrating?) is the fact that you can't save and restore games. You'll have to play it straight through once you start.

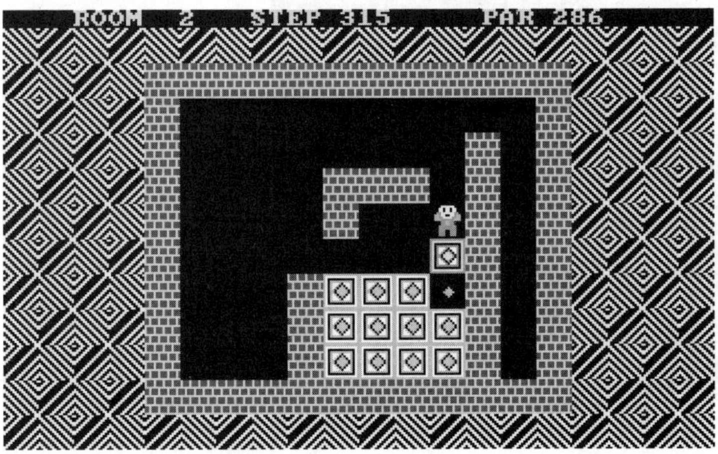

Figure 7-4
CRATES
This is one warehouseman who is sure to work overtime.

Nevertheless, the scenarios themselves are quite engaging, and we found that the game can grab your attention and keep you hooked for hours. Aside from our caveats above, we very much liked the overall implementation.

Directory:	\CHAP07\CRATES	Contact:	Mark Batchelor
To Play:	**CRATESD.EXE**		Summit Software
Date:	9-21-91		14567 Woodbine Avenue
Archive:	CRATES.ZIP		Gormley, Ontario
Registration:	$12		Canada L0H 1G0
			Tel: (905) 727-6964
			(after 4:30PM Eastern time)

CYBERBOX

by Doug Beeferman

Despite its apparent simplicity, Cyberbox (Figure 7-5) is a real mind-stretcher. You are the little white circle. Your goal is to get out of the room. You do it by pushing boxes aside. Some can be pushed horizontally, some can be pushed vertically. Some can be pushed in either direciton, and some boxes can't be moved at all. Others move by themselves if there's nothing blocking their way. Sounds easy enough, right? Heh heh heh heh. . . .

Don't be fooled. Cyberbox is more than challenging. It's frustrating, annoying, maddening, difficult, and just plain impossible. It's everything you want a puzzle to be.

There are no fancy graphics or sound effects here, but Cyberbox doesn't need them. This is a challenge for minimalists. There's no story to worry about. The puzzles are pure and unfettered.

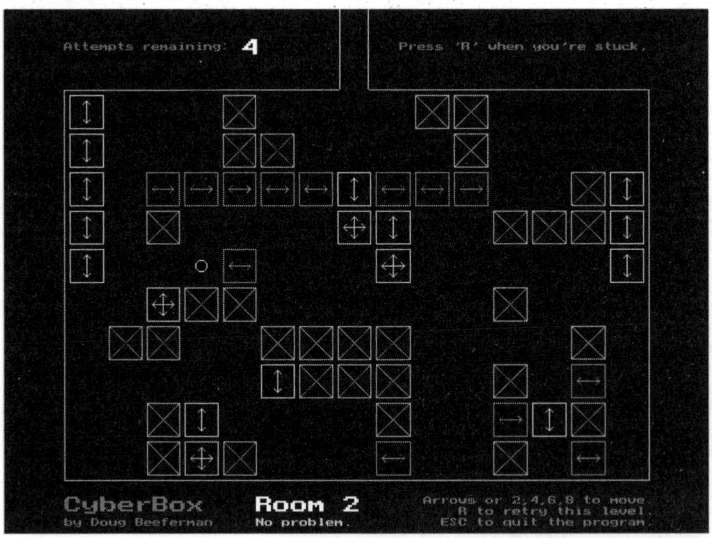

Figure 7-5
CYBERBOX
A metaphor for life. If you don't have pull, you have to *push*.

Cyberbox is a game of logic, position, and planning. You can spend more than a few evenings working your way through the challenges here, and it'll be good practice for Cyberbox 2.

Directory:	\CHAP07\CYBERBOX
To Play:	**CYBERBOX.EXE**
Date:	8-23-91
Archive:	CYBERBOX.ZIP
Registration:	$3

Contact: Doug Beeferman
904 W. Green St., Rm 506
Urbana, IL 61801

CYBERBOX 2

by Doug Beeferman

An obvious successor to Cyberbox, Cyberbox 2 (Figure 7-6) is a much more complex game, with a great deal more to do and discover. Fortunately, the entire first level is a teaching level. Nevertheless, it's still tricky and there are places where you can get yourself good and stuck, so be careful.

This time, you're a little white dot. You are moving through a large, scrolling background, filled with boxes. As before, some can only be pushed horizontally, some can only be pushed vertically, some can be pushed in both directions, and some can't be pushed at all. Some move by themselves if nothing's in the way.

But this time, things are a lot more complicated. You're moving through a large maze-like environment and there are patches of ice and other hazards to watch out for. There are also hint globes here and there to help explain some of the elements of the game.

The graphics are still simple, but they're effective. Sometimes you just want to play a game, you don't want or need a whole story. Like Cyberbox, Cyberbox 2 is a minimalist environment, uncluttered and uncomplicated.

The puzzles, however, are something else. Don't make assumptions. Cyberbox 2 will hook you with its seeming simplicity, but you'll be hunched over your keyboard long into the night. This is harder than it looks.

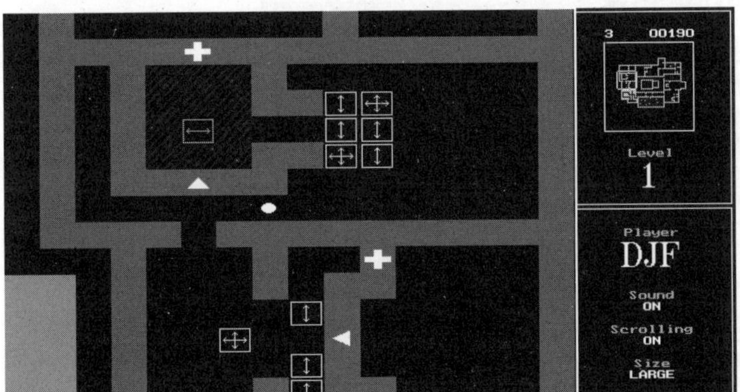

Figure 7-6
CYBERBOX 2
Can you find your way through the maze without getting boxed in?

Directory:	\CHAP07\CYBER2	Contact:	Doug Beeferman
To Play:	**C2.EXE**		904 W. Green St., Rm 506
Date:	8-11-92		Urbana, IL 61801
Archive:	CYBER2.ZIP		
Registration:	$7		

ANT RUN

by William Soleau

Ant Run, seen in Figure 7-7, is a little different from a standard pipe puzzle. Instead of laying pipe, you create tunnels for a red ant to crawl around in by turning the tunnel pieces so that they form a continuous tunnel. Once the ant crawls through a piece of tunnel, that piece becomes blocked and cannot be used again. If the ant crawls out of the maze through one of the holes at the edges of the ant hill, it will crawl back into the maze on the other side. The idea is to keep the ant moving as long as possible without making it run into a dead end.

Keep an eye on the inch meter on the right side of the screen. When the ant has crawled 20 inches, the blocked tunnel pieces will be cleared (and changed) the next time the ant crawls through a hole. This enables you to keep the ant moving for a longer period of time.

Here's a hint: use the Fast button on the left of the ant hill. As long as you hold down the mouse pointer while the arrow is on that button, the ant will move faster and collect twice as many points. There are at least two ways to use this button. The most obvious time when you should use this button is when you have a lengthy tunnel for the ant to use. Hold down the Fast button and watch the ant book through the tunnels, racking up points.

A less obvious time to use that button is when you know the ant will soon die. If you've arranged all the tunnel pieces you can, and the ant is destined to hit a dead end, make it run for it. With any luck, this will give you enough points to advance to the next level.

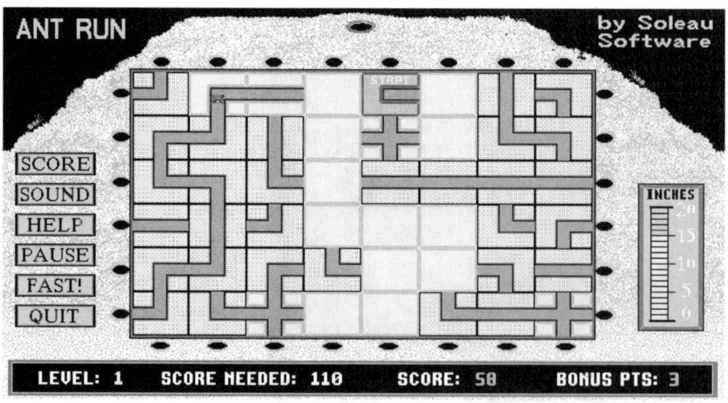

Figure 7-7
ANT RUN
Run along lil' ant...or else.

Directory: \CHAP07\ANTRUN
To Play: **ANTRUN.EXE**
Date: 3-1-93
Archive: ANTRUN.ZIP
Registration: $12 (provides unlimited levels)

Contact: Soleau Software
163 Amsterdam Avenue, Suite 213
New York, NY 10023
Tel: 212-721-2361
Fax: 212-873-4994

HEARTLIGHT

by Janusz Pelc

for Kids!

Heartlight (Figure 7-8) is a delicious surprise from Epic MegaGames. This one almost got away from us; we found it at the last minute before finishing the book. We took one look at it, and we knew it was a *must-have* game. Heartlight is terrific. It's one of the very best games of its kind that we've ever seen on a computer.

Heartlight is not quite a pushing and packing game. It's more of an outwitting-gravity game, but there's still quite a bit of pushing and packing involved and a great deal of strategy and planning.

Your job is to gather up all the hearts on the grassy playing field. If there's a metal sphere above you, it will fall down on you. If there's a balloon below you, it will push you up. If there's a hand grenade above you, it will fall down and blow up everything in a one-square radius.

The graphics, the animation, the music, the sound effects, everything about this game is superb, but what else would expect from Epic? But beyond that, there's an air of elegance and grace to this game.

Heartlight's puzzles appear simple enough. Each is constructed of only a few elements — grass, hearts, spheres, bombs, and balloons — yet each puzzle requires just enough thought and calculation to provide a genuine feeling of accomplishment when it's solved. And, appropriately enough, the game gives you an enthusiastic round of applause when you do deliver the little dwarf to the exit door of each screen.

Figure 7-8
HEARTLIGHT
Don't get boxed in. Plan ahead.

Almost every puzzle introduces either a new element, or a new interaction between elements, so as you proceed, you learn more and more about how the Heartlight world works. The puzzles become progressively more intricate.

What I particularly like about Heartlight is that, without ever being pedantic, it encourages that special kind of thinking needed for solving intricate problems one step at a time. This is a game that makes you smarter, just by playing it. And who doesn't want to get smarter? (If you get stuck, there's a file called HRTHNT.TXT which will help you with some of the more difficult screens.)

Dennis and I downloaded Heartlight from CompuServe one lazy Sunday afternoon and went through screen after screen of it together, trying to figure out each challenge together, slapping our foreheads simultaneously with every stupid mistake. After three hours, it was my turn to look at him and ask, "Hey, aren't we ever going to have dinner?"

(After he went to bed, I snuck back to the computer and tried again.)

Directory:	\CHAP07\HEART
To Play:	**HEART.BAT**
Date:	10-5-93
Archive:	HEART.ZIP
Registration:	$23 (includes shipping)

Contact: Epic MegaGames
10406 Holbrook Drive
Potomac, MD 20854
Tel: 301-299-3841
Toll-free: 800-972-7434
(orders only)
Fax: 301-299-3841

(The next morning, Dennis confessed, he'd snuck out of bed to watch me from the hallway.)

CHAPTER 8

STRATEGY

STRATEGY

The difference between a puzzle and a game of strategy is that in a puzzle, you are competing against the circumstances and conditions of the situation. In a game of strategy, you are competing against an opponent, so the circumstances and conditions are constantly changing.

In effect, a strategy game is a simulation of war. You are in a battle against a deadly opponent. He has no morals, no scruples. He will do whatever he has to do to destroy you completely. There is no truce possible here. The game must be played to its final outcome; either you or he will be destroyed. Here, at last, on your computer screen, is a place where the natural human tendency toward viciousness is finally an asset. You can work out all of your aggressions without having to worry that you are going to inflict a traumatic blow to the self-esteem of another human being.

Generally, a game of strategy involves the control of a defined playing field. You move or place your pieces to outflank and capture your enemy's pieces. The very best games of strategy are as deceptively simple as checkers or Reversi, only revealing their complexity when you bring your concentration to bear.

Creating a strategy game capable of challenging play usually involves elements of *artificial intelligence* that are not often present in any other kind of programming challenge. Actually, I have some problems with the term "artificial intelligence" primarily because we know so little about *genuine intelligence*. In fact, there is plenty of evidence, most of it on the front page of your newspaper, that there's no such thing as intelligence at all.

But what passes for artificial intelligence is generally a complex set of rules that a computer program uses for decision-making: *If Queen_Advantage is greater than 3, then do Capture, else do Run_Away. If Boardwalk_flag is true, then do Trade_Property, else if Ammunition is greater than 3000, then do Fight_Like_A_Cornered_Rat.* Whatever is appropriate.

Generally this rule-based decision-making can provide a very convincing simulation of intelligence within the defined boundaries of a computer game, which is why I think it's more appropriate to call it "simulated intelligence." The rules have to be broad enough to recognize all of the possible situations in a game. In chess, for instance, a program needs to be aware of opening book, midgame, and endgame situations, each of which require separate sets of rules.

The best strategy games allow you to set the "look-ahead" level as a way of controlling the "intelligence" of the game engine. This allows you to play the please-don't-hurt-me level while you are learning the game, and then graduate to the nightmare level when you start feeling overconfident.

We found a selection of strategy games that impressed us with both their attractiveness and their playability. You'll have a lot of fun with these.

IGO

by David Fotland

The ancient Japanese game of Go is often compared to chess. It is a game of position, in which strategy and careful planning play a large part. Despite its apparent simplicity, the game is deceptively complex. You can learn it in an afternoon, but it takes a lifetime to master. Indeed, most programmers consider it much more difficult to write a program that plays Go well than to write one that plays a strong game of chess.

The object of Go is to capture more territory on the board than your opponent. Pieces, or stones, are not moved on the board once they are placed. Stones are removed, however, if they are surrounded on four corners by the opponent's stones.

Igo—pronounced EEGO—is one of the very best implementations of Go we've ever seen (see Figure 8-1). The game play is quick and responsive; the graphics are elegant and attractive. Even better, Igo comes with an excellent tutorial that steps you through a series of sample games to teach you how the game is played, how pieces are captured, and even some of the complexities of advanced play.

Even if you've never taken the time to investigate Go before, you owe it to yourself to spend an afternoon with this implementation. It's well worth your time and you won't be sorry.

Directory: \CHAP08\IGO
To Play: **IGO.EXE**
Date: 12-05-93
Archive: IGO.ZIP
Registration: $0

Contact: Ishi Press International
76 Bonaventura Drive
San Jose, CA 95134
Tel: 408-944-9900
Fax: 408-944-9110

Figure 8-1
IGO
The ancient Japanese game Go takes a moment to learn, but a lifetime to master.

CHINESE CHECKERS

by ImagiSOFT, Inc.

What can you say about Chinese Checkers? Everybody knows it, everybody remembers it from their childhood. It's a terrific game.

And what can I say about ImagiSOFT's implementation of Chinese Checkers? (See Figure 8-2.) It's wonderful. It's classic Chinese Checkers, elegantly presented. The graphics are elegant, the play is strong, it's a lot of fun. I love it.

You can play any combination of humans and computer opponents that you choose. I prefer one-on-one, but the free-for-all can be exciting too. I would say that this game is commercial-quality, but that would be an insult. This game is *better* than many commercial products.

The registered version of Chinese Checkers allows you to save and restore a game in progress, undo previous moves, turn the animated icons on and off, and hear music and sounds through your Sound Blaster or Adlib Card.

Directory: \CHAP08\CHINESE
To Play: **CHINESE.EXE**
Date: 10-31-92
Archive: CC13.ZIP
Registration: $16.95 + $3 shipping

Contact: ImagiSOFT, Inc.
Computer Games Division
P.O. Box 13208
Albuquerque, NM 87192
Fax: 505-275-9697
CompuServe: 70632,1177
Prodigy: FSWM11A

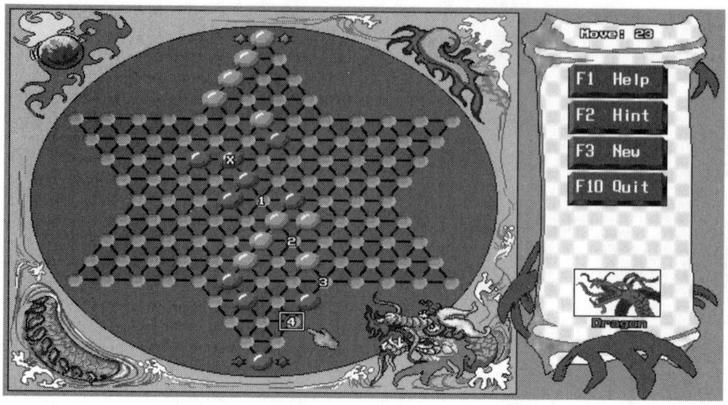

Figure 8-2
CHINESE CHECKERS
A classic game, beautifully done.

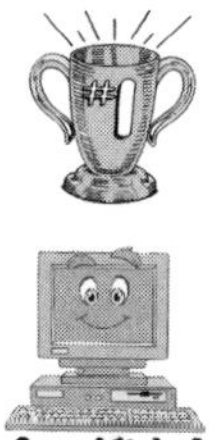

for Kids!

HEXXAGON I

by Jason Blochowiak and Abraham Edlin

illustration & animation by Don Glassford

digital and PC sound effects by Robert Prince

If you've ever played the 7-Up game, Spot, or its clone, Attax, then you know how to play Hexxagon (Figure 8-3). The important difference is that Hexxagon is played on a hexagonal field instead of a rectangular grid. The basic playing field also has three holes in it, near the center.

Your goal is to fill the playing field with as many of your pieces as possible. You have the red crystals, Craniac (the computer) has the chrome drops. Every time you place one of your red gems next to one of Craniac's pieces, his spheres are automatically transformed into scarlet jewels.

If you move one space over, you clone your gem, but if you jump, you leave a hole behind into which Craniac can put one of his pieces. Be careful.

That's pretty much it. The game is played until the board is filled. Like Reversi or Spot, the momentum of the game can shift back and forth with every move. The action is fast and intense. Fortunately, there's an Undo key, if you don't like your move.

The Craniac opponent has three levels of difficulty. The easy level is excellent for learning. The medium level provides a pretty challenging game. The Craniac *hard* level is . . . well, let's just say it has the advantage of being able to compute all the possibilities and never making any mistakes.

The game also has three levels of detail. At its highest level, the animation and sound effects are excellent. When Craniac's chrome spheres land next to your red gems, bolts of electric fire melt your scarlet jewel. When the reverse happens, when you capture Craniac's silvery balls, your jewel shoots a stream of frozen ice particles at each target.

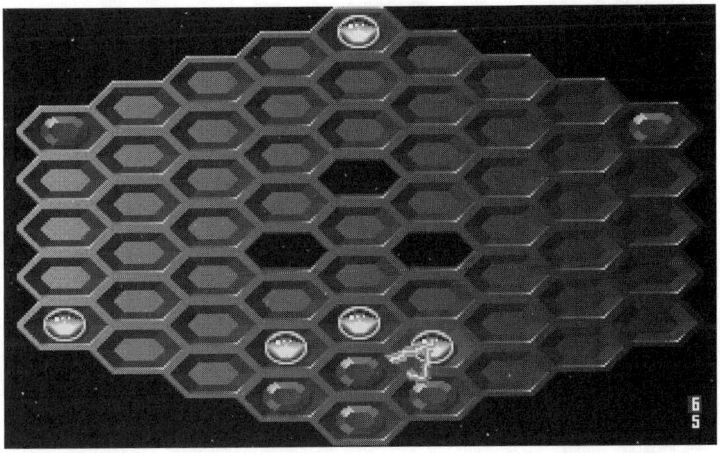

Figure 8-3
HEXXAGON I
You're going to have to think fast and carefully to beat the Craniac.

The best strategy is to fill in the edges of the board and then work your way inward, leaving no holes behind you. Your goal is to control as much territory as you can, so if you build a barrier of pieces that Craniac can't get past, all that territory behind it is yours to fill at your leisure (i.e., when Craniac runs out of places to move). It's also useful to count the number of pieces you'll gain on a given move against the number that Craniac will gain by countering.

Hexxagon is a terrific game for children, because the concepts are easy to understand, but don't underestimate it, it's also tricky enough to give adults a good challenge too. It's one of my favorites in this collection.

Directory:	\CHAP08\HEXXAGON
To Play:	**HEXX.EXE**
Date:	12-6-93
Archive:	HEXX.ZIP
Registration:	$20 + $2 shipping

Contact: Software Creations
26 Harris St.
Clinton, MA 01510
Tel: 508-368-8654
Fax: 508-365-7214

BEST 7 CARD

by J & J Gameware

It's like Kenny Rogers explained it, you've got to know when to hold 'em and know when to fold 'em. That's the challenge and appeal of poker. Riches or bankruptcy could be a card away, so you've got to play your hand carefully.

Best 7 Card, shown in Figure 8-4, is a nicely implemented version of seven card stud, a poker variant in which you are dealt seven cards one at a time (two face down, then four face up, and the last one down). Bets are placed at the start of each hand (that's an ante), then after the third through seventh cards are dealt. Whenever it's time to bet, the player with the best visible combination of cards gets to bet. Pay the amount of the bet to continue playing the hand. You can also increase the bet (raise) if you're confi-

Figure 8-4
BEST 7 CARD
Nowadays ya can't even hide a card up yer sleeve.

dent or quit your hand (fold) if you're not. After the final round of betting, the player with the best five-card poker combination wins the hand and the pot.

In the shareware version you play against three unique characters, and the registered version offers even more opponents. Bonnie Bomber is a librarian from Arkansas, "Vegas" Vinnie Botski is an IRS special agent, and Gertie Grabbit is a retired CIA agent. Each of you starts with $1000, and the game ends when you either lose all your money or win everyone else's.

At the start of the game, you can opt to view instructions if you desire. When deciding on how much to bet, keep in mind that Best 7 Card uses a standard 52-card deck. You might try bluffing occasionally; when your hand looks lousy, don't automatically fold. In our games, the opposition (especially "Vegas" Vinnie) didn't show much stomach for large bets and often folded. Besides, unlike the real thing, when you lose big money here, you don't risk a stay in the poorhouse.

Directory:	\CHAP08\BEST7CRD	Contact:	J & J Gameware
To Play:	**BEST7CRD.EXE**		P.O. Box 327
Date:	2-15-94		Hammond, IN 46320
Archive:	BEST7CRD.ZIP		
Registration:	$15.00 + 3.00 S &H		

CHAPTER 9

ACTION ADVENTURES

ACTION ADVENTURES

The largest and most popular category of game in this collection is the scrolling-action adventure — and for good reason. The scrolling-action adventure is played in real time; it's like playing an animated cartoon. The characters can have real personalities, the backgrounds are large and sophisticated, there is usually an engaging sound track, and the challenges and puzzles are often challenging enough to require *serious* concentration.

Generally, a scrolling-action game stars an animated character who operates against an environment too large to fit on your monitor. The scene scrolls smoothly across the screen as the character explores it, usually side to side, sometimes up and down as well.

You move the character with mouse, joystick, or arrow keys on the keyboard. Usually, you use the CONTROL key to jump and the ALT key to shoot — that is, if your character has a weapon. Sometimes not.

The game background is often multilayered with lots of treasures, bonuses, weapons, health, and keys that let you unlock more parts of the maze. Usually, the maze is populated by monsters, aliens, mutants, zombies, and assorted other things that slither, slide, creep, and crawl, all of which will happily eat you, dismember you, slime you, disintegrate you, or sometimes just knock you silly.

The scrolling-action game is a hybrid of all the classic game elements: mazes, puzzles, and arcade action. It's Nethack in real time, with graphics and animation. It's Pac Man with a personality and a plot. It's an arcade game and an adventure, both at the same time. I think that's why scrolling-action games have such widespread appeal. They're all the other games all in one place.

The first scrolling-action game on the PC was Captain Comic, which we've happily included here. It's still an engaging diversion. Since the days when Captain Comic first appeared, a multitude of other scrolling-action games have come down the channel, and we winnowed through them carefully. Most are wonderful. Most allow you to set the level of difficulty at which you want to play. One game even has a "granny" switch, which allows you to slow down the animation if you don't have the reflexes of a thirteen-year-old.

The very best scrolling-action games allow you to take a few hits without getting kicked back to the beginning. Getting killed is always a break in the flow of the game. The very best designers understand this; they want the game to be fun, so they give you every opportunity to avoid premature discorporation.

In most of the games we've included, your health is monitored as a percentage. Every hit costs you points. When your health hits zero, you die. This is a much more interesting way of handling the risk factor in a game because it allows you to practice serious resource management as you play. This creates much more depth to every life-threatening decision. Should you go hand-to-hand with the mutoid slimeball or should you leap for the restorative apple first?

You're going to have a lot of fun with these games. Don't forget to dust the television set before you sell it.

CAPTAIN COMIC

by Michael A. Denio

Captain Comic (Figure 9-1) is a landmark game. This was the very *first* scrolling-action game for MS-DOS. It was the breakthrough game. It was the camel's nose in the tent. It was (and still is) extremely popular. Everybody who saw it, wanted it. And every game designer who saw it was immediately inspired to new heights. Literally. Captain Comic was the first olive out of the bottle. Now, everybody is doing scrolling-action

Figure 9-1
CAPTAIN COMIC
Can you make this jump?

games, but Captain Comic was the first, and he will always hold a special place in our hearts.

Although Captain Comic looks easy enough at first glance, it is actually a very challenging game to play. It's mostly a jumping game, but the jumps have to be carefully calculated. As you walk from one end of the world to the other, you have to jump over rocks and trees and holes. You have to get the key to the exit door and you have to watch out for birds (and other critters) that will attack you and cost you health points.

As you go, you gather tools: shields, extra fireballs (cans of Blastola Cola), corkscrew bombs, jumping boots, lanterns, and wands. You get an extra life every time you earn 50,000 points or find a shield with your shield energy intact. Your goal is to find all three treasures: rare gems, rare coins, and a jeweled crown.

Here's a hint. When you get the key at the right end of the first level, don't go into the door immediately below it. Keep going toward the right and enter the next door instead.

Directory: \CHAP09\COMIC
To Play: **COMIC.EXE**
Date: 10-20-89
Archive: COMIC.ZIP
Registration: $20

Contact: Michael A. Denio
2906 William's Grant
Sugar Land, TX 77479

for Kids!

ELFLAND

by Carl Erikson

Although Elfland (Figure 9-2) looks like it's only for children, don't be fooled; it can be just as challenging to an adult. In fact, I never did find out how to reach the Grand Elf at the top of the tree.

This time, you're an elf, and although Elfland is protected by high fences, there is still a terrible danger from the trolls on the other side. You have been summoned by the Grand Elf, who will tell you how to get past the walls, so you can defeat the trolls. Single-handedly, of course.

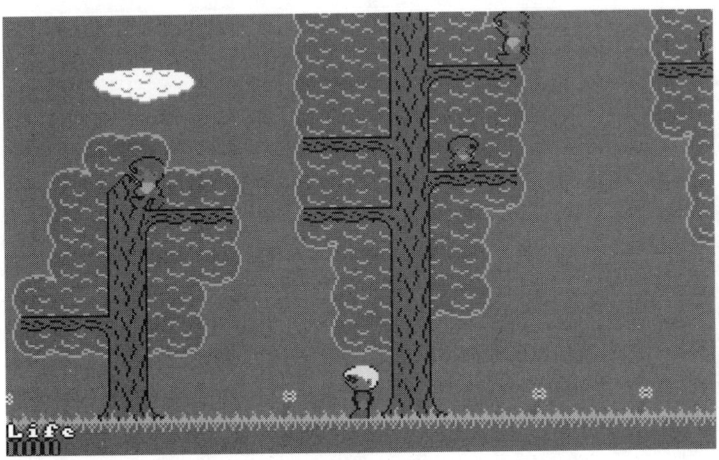

Figure 9-2
ELFLAND
Not just for children, Elfland can be very challenging.

Elfland is primarily a jumping game. You jump from tree branch to tree branch. You can also jump up onto clouds. Whenever you meet another elf, or other friendly person (like a cloud), you get a hint or further instructions. Although adults might find the difficulty of some of the jumps a little frustrating, this is an excellent adventure for younger gamers.

Directory:	\CHAP09\ELFLAND	Contact:	Carl Erikson
To Play:	**ELF1.EXE**		310 Edgemeer Place
Date:	10-19-92		Oberlin, OH 44074
Archive:	ELF.ZIP		
Registration:	$22 (for both episodes, includes shipping)		

for Kids!

PICKLE WARS

by Karen Crowther

Well, it had to happen. After everything else, the Earth has finally been invaded by sinister alien pickles. If your parents ever told you that you had to finish your salad or there would be no dessert, this is the game for you. At last, a chance to take revenge on all those terrible vegetables.

What can you say about a game that makes you laugh, even while it challenges you? (Check out Figure 9-3.) Warlike aliens resembling giant dill pickles have invaded the peaceful planet of Arcadia. Your job is to arm yourself with a SaladShooter and do battle with the dreaded Pickles. The SaladShooter tosses sliced cucumbers at the alien Pickles, which causes them to faint. You can play as either Dave or Linda, depending on which sex you feel is more heroic. Your goal is to find the Depository of Ancient Weapons, and ultimately the Doomsday Machine itself.

This is a multilevel, scrolling-action game. The graphics are state-of-the-art, with parallax scrolling. The view through the windows provides a nice feeling of depth when you move. The sound effects and music are equally superb. The action is fast enough to be challenging, but not so fast as to be impossible to play.

Figure 9-3
PICKLE WARS
If you don't finish your salad, it will finish you.

Some of the puzzles require a bit of work, but fortunately, the game provides you with excellent hints as you play. This is a game for both children and adults. But remember, if you don't finish all your salad, you don't get to play Pickle Wars.

Directory: \CHAP09\PICKLE
To Play: **PW1.EXE**
Date: 1-20-94
Archive: PICKLE.ZIP
Registration: $33 (for all three episodes, includes shipping)

Contact: MVP Software
1035 Dallas SE
Grand Rapids, MI 49507-1407
Tel: 616-245-8376
Order: 800-968-9684
Fax: 616-245-3204

for Kids!

GOD OF THUNDER: FIRST EPISODE

Programming by Ron Davis

Graphics by Gary Sirois

Level design by Adam Pederson

God of Thunder (Figure 9-4) isn't a scrolling-action adventure, because the backgrounds don't scroll. Instead, you journey through a series of playing fields, most of them containing combinations of arcade and puzzle challenges. God of Thunder is one of the very best animated adventures we've seen; it's a little like playing Hack or Rogue, but with terrific graphics added.

This is a wonderful game for children because of its many fanciful elements. (The hero can even have lunch at a restaurant with familiar-looking golden arches.) In fact, it's probably a *better* game for children than adults; Dennis solved several of the problems that stumped me.

Figure 9-4
GOD OF THUNDER
This must be Maxwell's Silver Hammer. It always comes back.

God of Thunder has many different kinds of monsters to fight. Fortunately you have a magic hammer that comes back to you every time you throw it. And every time you defeat a monster, you get a jewel or a magic potion. There are a lot of friendly folk in this world too, who will give you hints or advice when you talk to them — except for one old goat who insists on being left alone.

There are many different kinds of problem to solve here. Sometimes you have to find a key or push the right switch if you want to open a door. Sometimes you have to push blocks in front of spitting serpents. Sometimes you have to find your way through a difficult maze. And sometimes, you have to punch out annoying little red tribbles (or whatever they are) who insist on getting in your way.

What makes God of Thunder so much fun is that it combines many of the best kinds of puzzles and challenges all in one game. The animation, music, and sound effects are all state-of-the-art. This is a marvelous game. We love it.

Directory:	\CHAP09\GOT
To Play:	**GOT.EXE**
Date:	2-14-94
Archive:	GOT.ZIP
Registration:	$32 (for all three episodes, includes shipping)

Contact: Software Creations
26 Harris St.
Clinton, MA 01510
Orders: 508-368-8654
Fax: 508-365-7214
BBS: 508-365-7036

CHAPTER 10

COMMANDER KEEN

COMMANDER KEEN

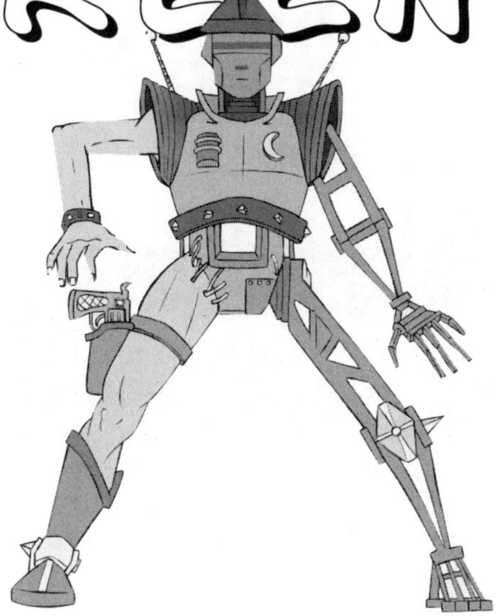

Although the gaming geniuses at ID Software are better known for their 3D action games, Wolf 3D and Doom, they are also responsible for a series of scrolling-action games that have been very big hits with children and adults alike.

It began with John Carmack. One night, he had an idea that it might be possible to use EGA graphics to create a scrolling background. By the following morning, Carmack, Tom Hall, and several others had created a one-level demonstration game. After a couple of false starts, that game eventually evolved into the first adventures of Commander Keen.

In real life, Commander Keen is actually Billy Blaze, an animated little boy with an imagination big enough to build a spaceship in his own backyard. Wearing only pajamas and a Green Bay Packers helmet, Commander Keen battles bizarre aliens all over the galaxy. In Keen Dreams, also known as the "lost adventure of Commander Keen," he even goes to war against malignant fruits and vegetables. Students of pop culture will recognize the influence of Chuck Jones and Bill Waterston here.

COMMANDER KEEN: INVASION OF THE VORTICONS

by John Carmack, John Romero, and Jason Blochowiak

for Kids!

Written by ID Software, distributed by Apogee, this first adventure introduces eight-year-old Billy Blaze, who has built his own spaceship out of household appliances. When he dons his brother's football helmet, he becomes *Commander Keen!* (Seen in Figure 10-1.)

Figure 10-1
COMMANDER KEEN: INVASION OF THE VOTRTICONS
No, this isn't Duck Dodgers or Spaceman Spiff.

In episode one, while Billy is exploring the monuments of Mars, the evil Vorticons steal valuable parts out of his spaceship. It is his job to visit each of the separate monuments and regain the missing pieces. Otherwise, he will never get home again!

Primarily, this is a *jumping* game. You need to figure out how to get from one ledge to the next. Some are a little too high or a little too far for you to leap to them from below or from the side, so you have to find a way to a ledge above, so you can jump down to them. There's a great deal of skill and coordination involved. Fortunately, the game has three different skill levels, so you can start out easy and work your way up to the harder levels.

Compared to some of the more recent games in this collection, this first Commander Keen adventure might look a little sparse, but don't let appearances fool you; the game is as challenging and as involving as any of the more sophisticated efforts that followed after.

Directory:	\CHAP10\VORTICON
To Play:	**KEEN1.EXE**
Date:	1-1-91
Archive:	KEEN1.ZIP
BBS Archive:	\CHAP10\VORTICON\BBS
Registration:	$40 (for all three episodes, includes shipping)

Contact: Apogee Software
P.O. Box 496389
Garland, TX 75049
Tel: 800-GAME-123

COMMANDER KEEN: GOODBYE GALAXY

by John Carmack, John Romero, and Jason Blochowiak

for Kids!

If it isn't one thing, it's another. This time, eight-year-old Billy Blaze, aka Commander Keen, has gotten himself into *serious* trouble.

The nasty alien Shikadi have captured the Gnosticenes of the planet Gnosticus and . . . oh, heck, you know the rest. Commander Keen has to fight his way past the thingies and the beasties and the whatchamacallits, rescue the whozis, and defeat the whatzis.

Fortunately, Keen has his pogo stick with him this time, which increases his jumping ability. Hit the (ALT) key to activate the pogo stick. If you run and jump and hit the pogo stick all at the same time, you can blast off at an angle and get a lot of extra height, but this does take practice. Of course nothing good ever comes easy. Read the documentation for more hints.

More importantly, the emphasis of the game is not entirely on jumping strategies anymore. There is much more interaction with the various critters and the player has to be a lot more careful and a lot more calculating to get through each set of tasks. Plus, as you will see, the animation in Goodbye Galaxy (see Figure 10-2) is more sophisticated than in the first Keen adventure. For instance, if Keen can't quite jump onto a ledge, he can still grab on by his fingertips and pull himself up.

As an extra bonus, this game includes a mini-game called Paddle War, which is just like the very first video game ever invented, Pong. Ask your grandma about Pong. She probably played it on her kerosene-powered PC.

Directory:	\CHAP10\GALAXY
To Play:	**KEEN4E.EXE**
Date:	2-1-92
Source:	KEEN4.ZIP
BBS Archive:	\CHAP10\GALAXY\BBS
Registration:	$40 (for all three episodes, includes shipping)

Contact: Apogee Software
P.O. Box 496389
Garland, TX 75049
Tel: 800-GAME-123

A commercial game starring Commander Keen, Aliens Ate My Baby Sitter, is also available. You can find it in software stores, or you can order it direct from Apogee.

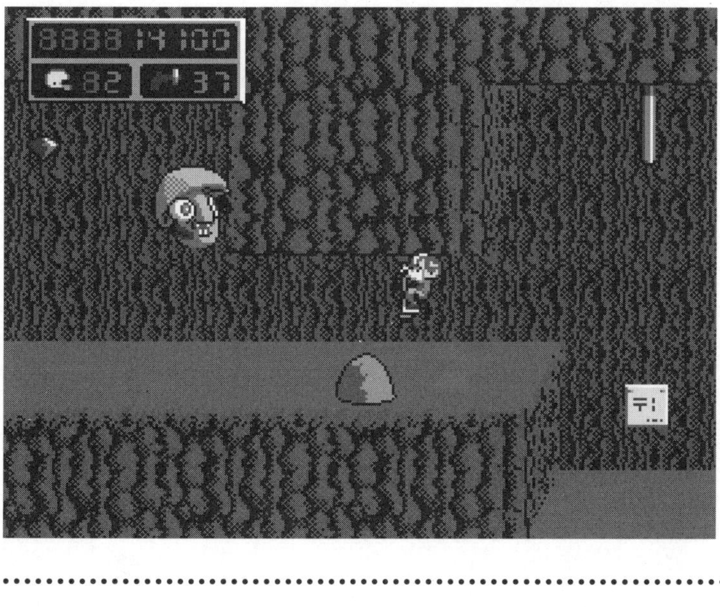

Figure 10-2
COMMANDER KEEN: GOODBYE GALAXY
Toto, I don't think we're in Kansas anymore. . . .

CHAPTER II

DUKE NUKEM

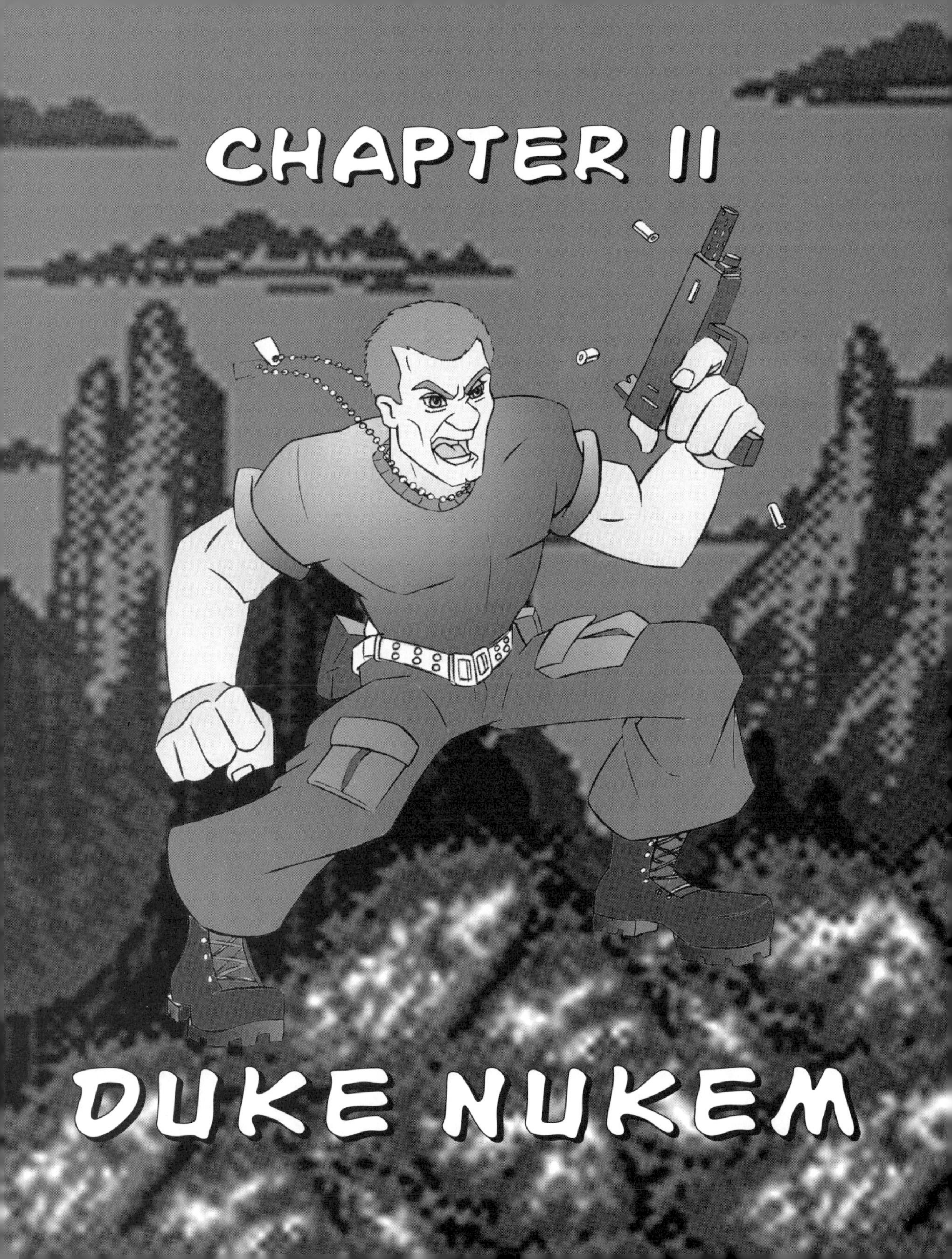

DUKE NUKEM

There are a lot of terrific scrolling-action games in the shareware channels. But the one that sets the standard of excellence for all the others is Duke Nukem. One of the most popular and enduring shareware games ever, Duke has been a favorite of gamers since he first blipped onto a computer screen.

Spend an afternoon or six with Duke, and you'll see why. Duke ain't no ordinary hero. He's... well, he's *Duke Nukem!*

DUKE NUKEM

programmed by Todd Replogle

graphics by Jim Norwood, Allen H. Blum III, George Broussard

produced by Scott Miller

Duke Nukem (shown in Figure 11-1) was first released in June of 1991. It climbed immediately onto the Shareware Top 10 list, where's it's remained ever since. No other shareware program (of any type) has been this enduring and popular. You only have to play Duke Nukem to see why. It's a well-crafted, scrolling-action adventure with attractive graphics, interesting challenges, and a terrific balance of risk and reward.

Dr. Proton and his army of techbots have taken control of Earth's largest city. Duke Nukem is Earth's final chance. Armed only with his pistol and his attitude, Duke must parachute into the city, track down the nefarious Dr. Proton and put a stop to his evil plans. Dr. Proton has several nuclear reactors to provide power for his techbots. Duke

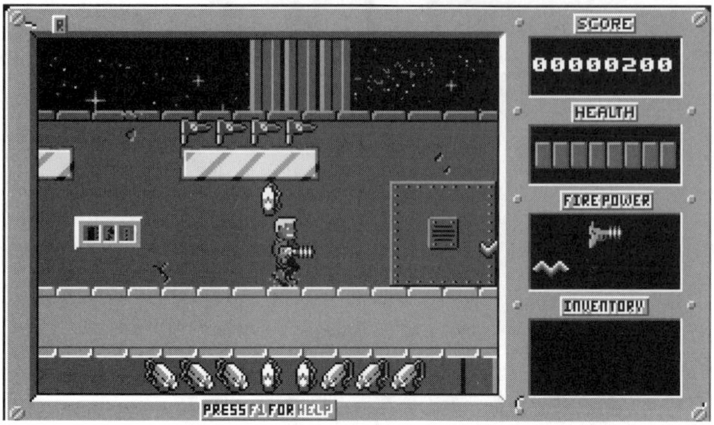

Figure 11-1
DUKE NUKEM
If it moves, shoot it. If it's thinking about moving, shoot it. Just to be on the safe side, shoot it.

must find and destroy them. Dr. Proton also has cameras watching Duke everywhere, so Duke must destroy every camera on the level to win a secret bonus.

The arrow keys control Duke's movements. The ↑ key is the action-key which allows Duke to insert keys in doors, and operate elevators, and other things like that.

Duke is armed with a nuclear pistol, so you should have quite a bit of firepower at your disposal, but Duke himself will need food and soft drinks to keep his health up, so you have to grab all the soda and turkeys you can find. Sometimes these things are hidden in boxes. Extra pistols, for instance, will increase Duke's firepower. Boots will increase his jumping ability. Duke has unlimited lives, but every time Duke dies, you have to restart the level, so be careful.

This disk will *not* self destruct in five seconds.

Directory:	\CHAP11\DUKE1	Contact:	Apogee Software
To Play:	**DN1.EXE**		P.O. Box 496389
Date:	11-1-91		Garland, TX 75049
Archive:	DUKE1.ZIP		Tel: 800-GAME-123
BBS Archive:	\CHAP11\DUKE1\BBS		
Registration:	$35 (for all three episodes)		

DukeMap
by David Bollinger

If David Bollinger isn't the world's number one Duke Nukem fan, then he's probably way ahead of whoever's in second place. DukeMap (Figure 11-2) is his utility for peeking into the data files for the Duke Nukem game, and seeing how each level is laid out.

DukeMap works on all three episodes and can display any level on the screen, or send the map to your printer for a hard copy version. Generally, you should only use

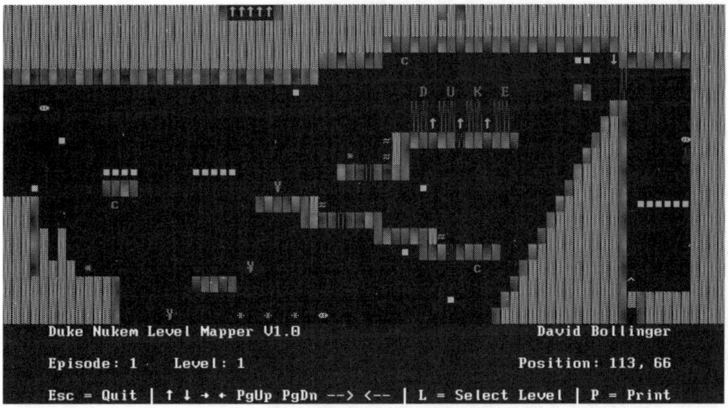

Figure 11-2
DUKEMAP.EXE
A Duke Nukem mapping utility.

the maps if you get stuck during the game. The maps are also useful for discovering areas you may have missed the first time through.

The program is easy enough to use; just copy it into the same directory with Duke Nukem, then type **DUKEMAP** and press (ENTER).

One important suggestion here. If you're going to use DukeMap, send your registration fee to Apogee and get all three levels of Duke Nukem. Why? Because if you're that determined a Duke Nukem player, then you should pay for the game you're enjoying so much.

Directory:	\CHAP11\DUKE1\MAPS	Contact:	David Bollinger
To Start:	**DUKEMAP.EXE**		P.O. Box 894
Date:	10-14-91		Denair, CA 95316
Archive:	DUKEMAP.ZIP		

DUKE NUKEM II

programming by Todd J. Replogle

level designer Allen H. Blum III

produced by George Broussard

As terrific as the first Duke Nukem adventure was, Duke Nukem II (Figure 11-3) is at least twice as good. Or maybe even better than that. This is a shoot-*everything*-that-moves game, with spectacular sound effects, animation, and graphics. In fact, even if it's not moving, you should probably shoot it anyway, just in case it's thinking about moving.

The game environment is the usual stew of deranged science fiction ingredients: evil alien thingies, clawing robots, slime-green mutants, pipes of dripping acid, carnivorous blobs in glass tanks, exploding traps, lethal bombs, super weapons, teleportation

Figure 11-3
DUKE NUKEM II
Duke is back, meaner than ever. If mayhem has a middle name. . . .

pods… all the usual stuff. Yes, there's a story to this, but it hardly matters. When you're that busy shooting everything that moves, you don't stop to read the fine print.

This time, Duke has been captured by aliens who want to drain his brain. All he has to do is escape from their UFO and then… . You'll discover that there's an awful lot to this game, much more than can be seen in a single session. Every level has a different scenario, and they are all wild and unusual. You can work at this for quite a while and still not see everything there is to see.

Duke is still made of pretty stern stuff. It takes an awful lot to hurt him, let alone kill him. And that's pretty useful, because there are a lot of ways to get killed in this game. Fans of the original game will be happy to see that Duke still flips when he jumps, and he can still walk hand over hand across pipes, chains, and ropes, but now he has the new ability to shoot down while he does so. Duke can also crouch, duck, and shoot upward. H'ray for Duke!

Duke has four weapons to use here: a blaster, a laser cannon, missiles, and a flamethrower. The blaster can sometimes be used in rapid-fire mode. The missiles will shoot through *anything*. The flamethrower, when aimed downward, propels Duke upward like a jetpack! Duke is a one-man Armageddon. Thank goodness he's a good guy. Can you imagine having to fight someone like him?

Directory: \CHAP11\DUKE2
To Play: **NUKEM2.EXE**
Date: 12-1-93
Archive: DUKE2.ZIP
Registration: $35 (for all *four* episodes)

Contact: Apogee Software
P.O. Box 496389
Garland, TX 75049
Tel: 800-GAME-123

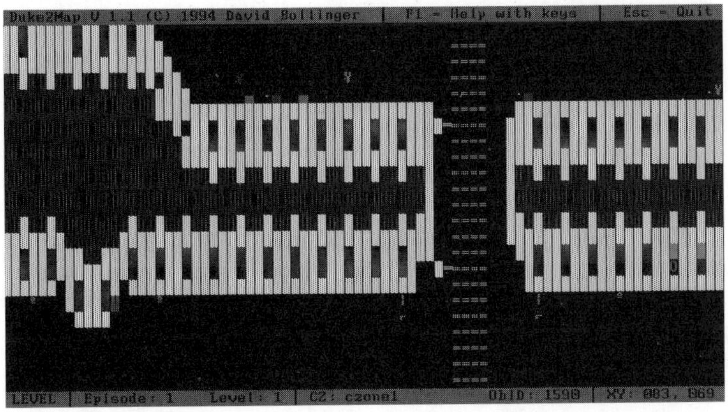

Figure 11-4
DUKE2MAP
A Duke Nukem II mapping utility.

Duke2Map
by David Bollinger

Once again, David Bollinger demonstrates dedication to Duke Nukem above and beyond the call of duty. Duke2Map (Figure 11-4) is his utility for peeking into the data files for the Duke Nukem II game, and seeing how each level is laid out.

Duke2Map works on all three episodes of Duke Nukem II and can display any level on the screen, or send the map to your printer for a hard copy version. It even comes with configuration files for your laser printer.

Generally, you should only use the maps if you get stuck during the game. The maps are also useful for discovering areas you may have missed the first time through.

Directory:	\CHAP11\DUKE2\MAPS
To Start:	**DUKE2MAP.EXE**
Date:	1-22-94
Archive:	DUKE2MAP.ZIP
BBS Archive:	\CHAP11\DUKE2\BBS

Contact: David Bollinger
P.O. Box 894
Denair, CA 95316

CHAPTER 12

APOGEE SOFTWARE

APOGEE SOFTWARE

The more games we gathered for this book, the more we realized just how many great games have come from Apogee Publishing. Apogee Publishing has established itself as the leading publisher of shareware entertainment, releasing more top-notch games than any other company.

Apogee may be best known for its extensive library of scrolling-action games; Duke Nukem and Commander Keen are the most famous, and their newest, Halloween Harry, is even more impressive. The company also published the spectacular "shooter" game, Raptor. And . . . not to belabor the obvious, they have also released two of the very best 3D games, Wolfenstein 3D and Blake Stone.

When you pick up an Apogee shareware game, you're getting a *complete* episode. It isn't "cripple-ware." It isn't a demo. All ten levels are available, all the features of the full game are available. There isn't anything missing. You get to play the game as much as you want until you are absolutely *hooked*.

Because every Apogee game is part of a trilogy (or more), the next games in the series are the incentive to register. If the first game has grabbed your interest, you'll order the next episodes immediately. At a cost of $15 - $20 per episode, a great shareware game gives you more value for your entertainment dollar than just about anything else you can purchase.

This has made Apogee a top game publisher and other publishers are now following their lead. You'll find Apogee games throughout this collection. But this section has been set aside to focus on five of their very best scrolling-action games.

BIO MENACE

by Jim Norwood

(core game engine by ID Software)

Metro City has fallen under the attack of hideous mutants. You are Snake Logan, top CIA operative. While circling over the city on a recon mission, you're shot down by hostile forces and forced to crash land in the streets. Grabbing what supplies you can, you fight your way through the fierce pink slugs and dreadful dragons, freeing hostages and looking for the terrible Dr. Mangle who is behind this attack.

Bio Menace (Figure 12-1) is a Duke Nukem-style, shoot-everything scrolling-action adventure. (It definitely wins high marks from the local nine-year-old.) The graphics are excellent, and the music and sound effects are the highest quality. The game has three skill levels, so even your grandma can play.

Snake Logan is a weapons expert, and uses several throughout the game, including machine guns and hand grenades. The sound effects and animations when a monster is destroyed have a deliciously gory cartoon-like quality, kind of like watching Wiley E. Coyote go through a paper shredder.

In this game, you have several additional powers, including the *super plasma bolt* which can burn through a whole line of enemies at once, but it costs you a hit point of damage when you do, it's that powerful. You also have a *fire ball attack*, an *electron shield*, and an *invincibility burst*. You have to discover these while playing the game.

Directory:	\CHAP12\B-MENACE	Contact:	Apogee Software
To Play:	**BMENACE1.EXE**		P.O. Box 496389
Date:	8-24-93		Garland, TX 75049
Archive:	BMENACE.ZIP		Tel: 800-GAME-123
BBS Archive:	\CHAP12\B-MENACE\BBS		
Registration:	$35 (for all three episodes)		

Figure 12-1
BIO MENACE
Those furry pink things aren't tribbles, but you can shoot them anyway. I won't mind.

COSMO'S COSMIC ADVENTURE

by Todd J. Replogle, Allen Blum III, Stephen A. Hornback, and Robert Prince

for Kids!

What's green with red spots, has suction hands, and an overbite like Bart Simpson? Cosmo! A young alien with an unflappable demeanor.

Cosmo's parents have been kidnapped by strange alien creatures on an unfamiliar planet. Cosmo's Cosmic Adventure is an epic journey across a planet full of dangers and surprises. Can he save his parents in time?

Cosmo (Figure 12-2) can cling to walls and ledges and other vertical surfaces. The game itself has a powerful multi-scrolling graphics engine, similar to games found on dedicated systems like Sega Genesis and Super Nintendo. There are nineteen different musical themes and twenty different animated creatures.

This is a great game for children. Although adults might find some of the challenges a little daunting, children don't suffer from the same sensibilities and will happily tackle those most impossible challenges, including fighting you for the computer.

Directory:	\CHAP12\COSMO
To Play:	**COSMO1.EXE**
Date:	4-15-92
Archive:	COSMO1.ZIP
BBS Archive:	\CHAP12\COSMO\BBS
Registration:	$35 (for all three episodes)

Contact: Apogee Software
P.O. Box 496389
Garland, TX 75049
Tel: 800-GAME-123

Figure 12-2
COSMO'S COSMIC ADVENTURE
Not every hero needs a gun.

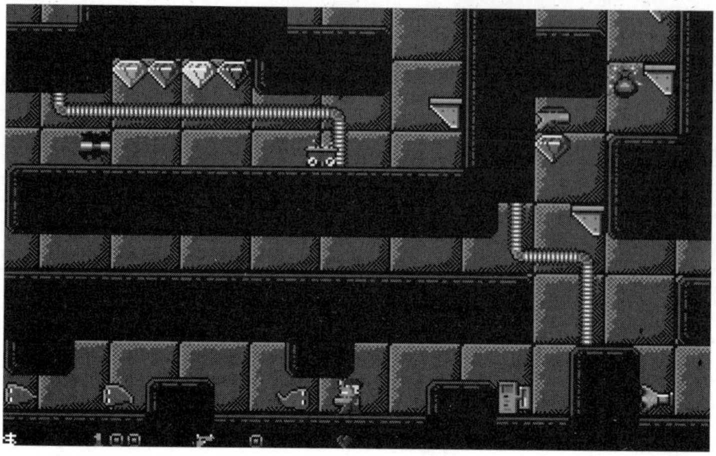

Figure 12-3
CRYSTAL CAVES
It's time to pickle your twibbles in your old kit bag.

for Kids!

CRYSTAL CAVES: TROUBLES WITH TWIBBLES

by Frank Maddin

Mylo Steamwitz rockets to the mysterious Crystal Caves of Altair to gather priceless artifacts and jewels. But the dwellers of the Crystal Caves sure are... well, troublesome. And Mylo soon finds that he has serious troubles with twibbles. (Hmm. Why does that title sound so familiar? And why do I keep thinking about quadro-triticale?)

This game, seen in Figure 12-3, is a remarkable little treasure. It is well designed, it has clever graphics and animation, the sound effects are appropriate, and the puzzles are hard enough to be challenging, but not so hard as to be impossible.

One of the nicer touches is that you can get killed as many times as you make mistakes without getting kicked out of the game. You will have to start a specific level over again if you get zinged three times, but there's no limit to how many times you can try.

You begin your adventure in the main mineshaft. There are sixteen separate mines. You have to enter all sixteen of them and gather all the jewels in each one before you can exit again. Some of the jewels are hidden and you have to bump your head against certain platforms to find them. If you grab a power pill, your space gun will become more powerful. To pass through a colored door, you need to pull the switch of the same color.

This is all fairly simple stuff, but it's so elegantly and gracefully implemented that the game is a definite winner. It's certainly one of the very best games in the scrolling-action genre. I like it because it isn't quite as bloodthirsty as some of the others, and all the different critters found throughout the Crystal Caves give the game an enchanting quality.

Directory: \CHAP12\CRYSTAL
To Play: **CC1.EXE**
Date: 10-23-91
Archive: CRYSTAL.ZIP
BBS Archive: \CHAP12\CRYSTAL\BBS
Registration: $35 (for all three episodes, includes shipping)

Contact: Apogee Software
P.O. Box 496389
Garland, TX 75049
Tel: 800-GAME-123

Figure 12-4
HALLOWEEN HARRY
A jet pack and a flamethrower. What more could you ask for? Life is good. Life is fine.

HALLOWEEN HARRY

by Tony Ball, Robert Crane, Steven Stamatiadis, and John Passfield

Halloween Harry (Figure 12-4) is my personal favorite of all the Apogee scrolling-action games. Although the challenges of the actual game seem tougher (to me) than most of the other Apogee adventures, the animation and sound effects are so attractive and clever that they set a new standard of excellence. The scrolling-action screens are among the best I've ever seen, and Harry himself is so personable, with so much attitude and expression in his movements, that he has much more character than the average computer game hero. In other words, this is a fun place to play.

Apogee says that Halloween Harry is the first of a new generation of games: *"A big-time production with no detail overlooked. Professional musical soundtrack, brilliant full-VGA graphics, nonstop animation, and impressive start-game and end-game cinematic animations."*

This time around... Earth is being taken over by aliens intent on turning human beings into mindless slave zombies. (Again?!!) Harry's job is to penetrate the alien ship which has burrowed itself under a high-rise city.

Harry has a wide selection of weapons at his disposal, including a spectacular flamethrower. His jet pack allows him to fly up and down to different levels of the map. But you have to be careful, because you can run out of fuel and ammunition very quickly if you don't manage your resources well.

In addition to the flamethrower, Harry can use weapons he finds during the game, including a photon cannon, guided missiles, grenades, shields, micro-nukes, and the very powerful Omega bomb. It's quite an arsenal. The smart bullets will bounce around the screen until they find their target; it's a lot of fun to watch.

Harry has terrific Sound Blaster music and sound effects, a built-in radar mode for tracking enemies, a cheat mode, three skill levels (in case grandma wants to play), and some of the best VGA graphics and animation ever seen in a scrolling-action game. Plus... when you register, you get three additional missions instead of two!

Halloween Harry also gets an enthusiastic two thumbs-up from the resident nine-year-old. If he had any more thumbs, he'd probably point them up too.

Directory: \CHAP12\HARRY
To Play: **HH1.EXE**
Date: 11-7-93
Archive: HARRY.ZIP
BBS Archive: \CHAP12\HARRY\BBS
Registration: $35 (for all four episodes)

Contact: Apogee Software
P.O. Box 496389
Garland, TX 75049
Tel: 800-GAME-123

MONSTER BASH

by Frank Maddin

Well, here's another fine mess you've gotten yourself into. This time, you're Johnny Dash and your dog Tex has been kidnapped by the evil Count Chuck. Monster Bash has more gruesome action than any other Apogee scrolling-action game. There are over eight megabytes of animated/scrolling graphics in all three monstrous episodes.

Although Monster Bash (Figure 12-5) is populated by zombies, vampires, creeping hands, and other ghouls, it's still (generally) suitable for children. The critters are more cartoon-like than scary. Impressionable children might find the theme too intense, but as they proceed through the game, they get to rescue all the dogs and cats that Count Chuck has trapped and this does provide a mitigating quality.

Johnny Dash is one of the most limber of all Apogee heroes. He can jump, climb, crawl, shoot his slingshot in several directions, fly a broom, and more. His super-charged slingshot can shoot rocks, rockets, fireballs, and a few other surprises. There are also more enemy creatures and monsters than seen in any previous Apogee game.

As with most of the other Apogee games, the local nine-year-old gives this one an enthusiastic rating.

Figure 12-5
MONSTER BASH
Night of the Living Nine-Year-Old. Lock up your zombies.

Chapter 12 Apogee Software

Directory:	\CHAP12\BASH	Contact:	Apogee Software
To Play:	**BASH.EXE**		P.O. Box 496389
Date:	5-25-93		Garland, TX 75049
Archive:	BASH.ZIP		Tel: 800-GAME-123
BBS Archive:	\CHAP12\BASH\BBS		
Registration:	$35 (for all three episodes)		

CHAPTER 13

EPIC MEGAGAMES

EPIC MEGAGAMES

And then there's Epic. As we gathered and selected games for this collection, we kept coming across the name Epic MegaGames, over and over and over again. And every time we did, we found a game that was unique and delightful. There's no such thing as a "typical" Epic game. Each one is different. Every one is special.

As you'll see.

BRIX

by Michael Riedel

Brix is both an arcade game and a puzzle experience. You'll need fast reflexes as well as all of your sly terrestrial cunning. Brix occurs on an abstract playing field inhabited by multiple objects of different shapes and colors. Whenever two or more matching objects are placed side by side, they both disappear.

Your job is to move the pieces around and clear the field of all objects. Believe me, it only looks simple. Considerable planning and forethought are necessary for solving every puzzle. And just to make things interesting, you're playing against the clock.

There are 112 levels in this unique game. Some of them contain lasers, elevators, boiling acid, antigravity, teleporters, and other surprising challenges to your problem-solving skills.

Brix (see Figure 13-1) is extremely well crafted. The graphics are beautiful, and if you have a sound card, the musical accompaniment is very impressive. Plus, whenever you succeed in solving a puzzle, you also get an enthusiastic round of cheers and applause.

This is a challenging and fascinating set of puzzles, and it sets a new standard for excellence in graphic arcade games.

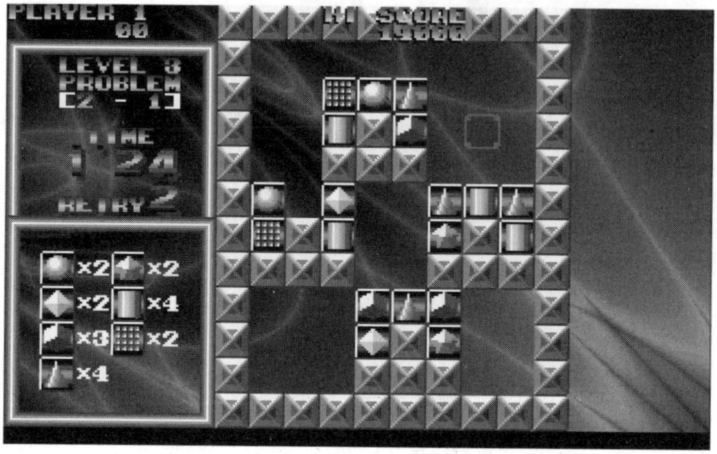

Figure 13-1
BRIX
Push the matching pieces together and make them disappear.

Directory:	\CHAP13\BRIX	Contact:	Epic MegaGames
To Play:	**BRIX1.EXE**		10406 Holbrook Drive
Date:	9-22-93		Potomac, MD 20854
Archive:	BRIX.ZIP		Tel: 301-299-3841
Registration:	$34 (for Brix and Brix 2, includes shipping)		Toll-free: 800-972-7434 (orders only)
			Fax: 301-299-3841

EPIC PINBALL

designed by James Schmalz

produced by Mark Rein

code by James Schmalz and Joshua Jensen

Wow! What can I say about one of the most amazing simulations I've ever seen on a computer? If you like pinball, you're going to *love* Epic Pinball. It looks and feels just like a real pinball machine on your desk. You can even tilt it if you're not careful. Wow!

Epic Pinball (Figure 13-2) is going to hook you. Playing is easy. You pull back the shooter by holding down the spacebar. When you release the spacebar, or when the spring is pulled all the way back, whichever happens first, the ball is fired into play. With a little practice, you'll have considerable control over how fast the ball is launched.

You can use either the ← and → keys or the left-SHIFT and right-SHIFT keys to work the flippers. You can also give the table a nudge by hitting the spacebar, but don't press it too long or you'll *tilt*. That's pretty much all you need to know to play, but winning is something else again. That's a matter of timing and reflexes.

There are three more pinball tables in game pack 1. You can see them, but you can't play them until you register. There are four more tables available in game pack 2. Each

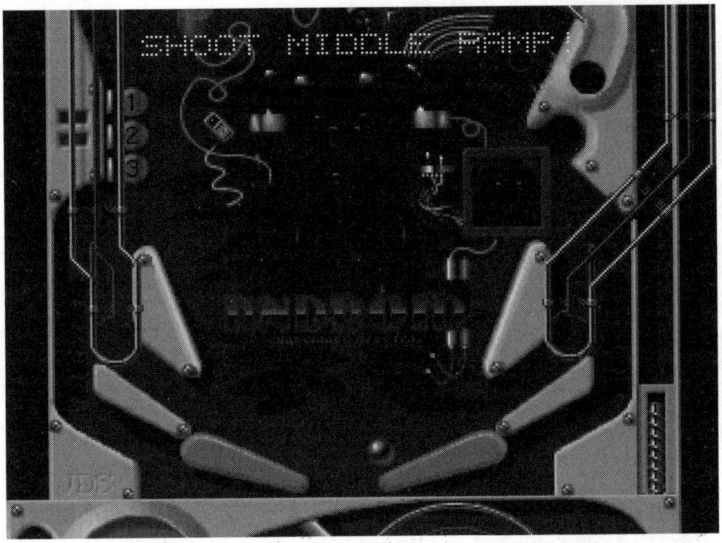

Figure 13-2
EPIC PINBALL
Who needs an arcade?
This is better.

table has its own unique set of rules and ways to earn bonuses. Be sure to read *all* of the documentation; if you do, you'll learn a very important secret.

Even if you're not a pinball fan in the arcades, you're still going to find this a lot of fun on your computer. Dennis and I like it more than real pinball machines. The realistic action is enhanced by terrific sound effects. As with all of the Epic games, the graphics are stunning and the music is wonderful.

Directory: \CHAP13\PINBALL
To Play: **PINBALL.EXE**
Date: 10-27-93
Archive: EPINBALL.ZIP
Registration: $33 (for either game pack 1 or 2, includes shipping)
$49 (for both game packs, includes shipping)

Contact: Epic MegaGames
10406 Holbrook Drive
Potomac, MD 20854
Tel: 301-299-3841
Toll-free: 800-972-7434 (orders only)
Fax: 301-299-3841

Just as we went to press, Epic released a new version of Epic Pinball, with a Super-Android table. You'll find it in the BONUS directory.

SOLAR WINDS

by James Schmalz
musical sound track by Dan Froelich

Solar Winds is a space-exploration adventure with some arcade elements. You are Jake Stone, bounty hunter. You pilot your starship all over the galaxy, looking for work and trying to keep out of trouble. But try as you might, trouble *will* come looking for you.

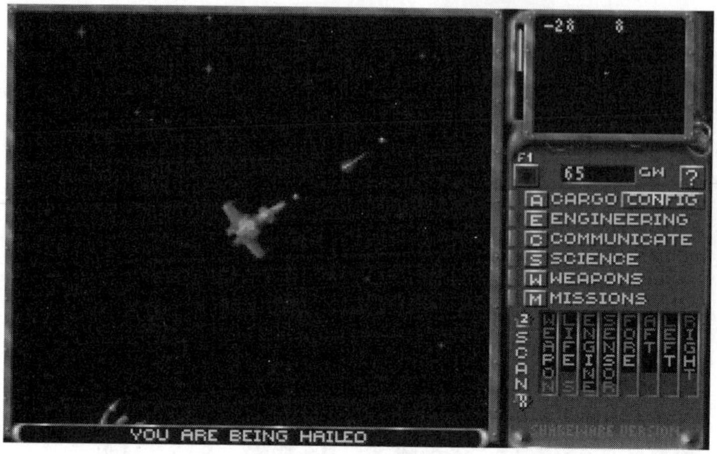

Figure 13-3
SOLAR WINDS.
Open Hailing Frequencies, Lieutenant....

Solar Winds (Figure 13-3) is *not* a shoot-em-up. Although there are plenty of opportunities for explosive action, the emphasis in this game is on the jobs you are offered, whether or not you accept them, how you carry them out, and ultimately, how much money you earn.

You will encounter many other starships in your travels. You can communicate with all of them or fight with them. If you try to fight with them, you're likely to play a very short game. On the other hand, if you're smart enough to attempt communication, the conversations can be very revealing. This is almost an interactive novel; the plot is well developed and you will discover more and more secrets as you play.

It's compelling and engrossing. Solar Winds is one of the reasons why this book was turned in late.

Directory: \CHAP13\SOLAR
To Play: **SOLAR1.EXE**
Date: 9-22-93
Archive: SOLAR.ZIP
Purchase: $34 (for both episodes)

Contact: Epic MegaGames
10406 Holbrook Drive
Potomac, MD 20854
Tel: 301-299-3841
Toll-free: 800-972-7434 (orders only)
Fax: 301-299-3841

JILL OF THE JUNGLE

programming and design by Tim Sweeney
artwork by John Pallett-Plowright and Joe Hitchens
musical sound track by Dan Froelich

Well, it's about time. Why should all the heroes be men? Why aren't there more games where women get to jump through mazes, hacking and slashing and killing all the monsters? Jill of the Jungle (Figure 13-4) is a chance for women to be as barbaric as their male counterparts. H'ray. Isn't equality wonderful?

Figure 13-4
JILL OF THE JUNGLE
You Tarzan, Me Jill. Me smash villains today. You stay home with Cheetah.

Jill is an excellent and very challenging game. You might find it a little harder than some other scrolling-action programs; I did, but then again, I'm not thirteen. Nevertheless, this game is definitely worth the effort. There's an excellent Sound Blaster sound track, and as a bonus, there's a "save and restore" feature. You can save your game to disk and resume play later at the same point. This is very useful for people who hate starting over.

Like other high-intensity scrolling-action games, Jill requires a lot of system resources. The documentation includes tips on how to get it running if you have problems.

Directory: \CHAP13\JILL
To Play: **JILL.BAT**
Date: 12-27-93
Archive: JILL.ZIP
Purchase: $34 (for all three episodes)

Contact: Epic MegaGames
10406 Holbrook Drive
Potomac, MD 20854
Tel: 301-299-3841
Toll-free: 800-972-7434 (orders only)
Fax: 301-299-3841

XARGON

by Allen Pilgrim
artwork by Joe Hitchens
musical sound track by Dan Froelich

Xargon is the male equivalent of Jill of the Jungle. The program is clearly built on the same game engine, but the game itself is a totally different environment. As with Jill, Xargon (Figure 13-5) is very challenging and will require a lot of practice.

As with all of the other products from Epic MegaGames, both the graphics and the sound are terrific. The animation is wonderful. As with Jill, there's a "save and restore" feature. You can save your game to disk and resume play later on at the same point. This is very useful for people like me who get killed a lot.

Figure 13-5
XARGON
A man's gotta do what a man's gotta do.

Like other high-intensity scrolling-action games, Xargon requires a lot of system resources. The documentation includes useful tips on how to get it running if you have problems.

Directory:	\CHAP13\XARGON
To Play:	**XARGON.BAT**
Date:	1-1-94
Archive:	XARGON.ZIP
Purchase:	$34 (for all three episodes)

Contact: Epic MegaGames
10406 Holbrook Drive
Potomac, MD 20854
Tel: 301-299-3841
Toll-free: 800-972-7434 (orders only)
Fax: 301-299-3841

One part of Xargon is a particularly frustrating labyrinth. A map of the labyrinth is provided (LABSOL.GIF) in the subdirectory CHAP08\XARGON\MAPS. To view LABSOL.GIF, or any GIF file, you'll need a GIF file viewer. Many commercial graphic packages — such as Adobe Photoshop, Aldus Photostyler, HiJaack, and Collage — provide this feature. A number of shareware packages also allow GIF viewing. A section in the back, "About This Book," provides a list of shareware sources. These distributors can supply you with such shareware graphic programs as Image Alchemy, JPEG View, PICEM, File Buddy, or others.

CHAPTER 14

SHOOTERS

SHOOTERS

The very first shooter game was an arcade machine called Space Invaders. It was a summer hit, pulling quarters out of pockets almost as if they were magnetized. And then, just as fast, it was superseded by a host of imitations and spinoffs that went far beyond the original concept.

In Space Invaders, you had four rows of crudely drawn alien spaceships zig-zagging back and forth across the screen, each time coming lower and lower, and all the time shooting missiles down at you. Since then, shooter games have evolved into some very spectacular challenges, as you are about to see.

We found a very large number of shareware shooter games, most of them excellent, but many more than we could include, so we had to be very rigorous in our selection. Even so, we still ended up with more shooter-type games than we expected.

Shooter-type games are most popular with the under-18 age group; that is, those who do not need excessive doses of caffeine to reach turbo mode. All of these games require speed-of-light reflexes and the hand-eye coordination of a ninja. The goal is to shoot everything you can until you're wired so tight you're hyperventilating.

Also in their favor, shooter games are without significant redeeming social value.

DESERT RAID
by COPYSOFT

Skunny Hardnut is no ordinary special agent. He gets only the toughest missions, because he's the best of the best. He's also a squirrel. In Desert Raid, Skunny's drawn a particularly nasty job: armed with only a bi-plane and precious few bombs, he must fight through the armies of Sadman Insane and destroy the evil dictator's plans for global domination.

Playing Desert Raid (see Figure 14-1) is easy enough, it's walking away from it that's not. To start a game, select "Play Game" from the opening menu. When the game begins, use the up and down arrows to choose an objective, then press ENTER. You can select either Headquarters or the Airport, but novices may want to pick the closer target (the airport).

Flying through hostile enemy territory, you've got to destroy just about anything that moves: helicopters, planes, anti-aircraft guns, rockets, and Sadman's other "weapons of mass destruction." Use the arrow keys to maneuver the plane, press the SPACE BAR to fire the guns, and press ALT to drop bombs. Along the way you can collect parachuting nuts and bombs to increase your health and ammo. You've got a finite number of bombs, so use them wisely. And remember to avoid obstacles, like trees, fortresses, and surface-to-air missiles.

Desert Raid is the self-described "Mother of the Father of the Grandmother of all Battles." While the lineage might be confusing, this game is a member of an entertaining family of games featuring Skunny Hardnut: Special Agent for Hire. You'll find more of these in the CD BONUS directory.

Figure 14-1
DESERT RAID
If you wanted the friendly skies, this ain't it.

Directory:	\CHAP14\DESRAID	Contact:	COPYSOFT (Headquarters)
To Play:	**DESERT.EXE**		Rue de Menuisier
Date:	10-8-93		1200 Bruxelles
Archive:	DESRAID.EXE		Belgium
Registration:	$20		Tel: 32-2-772-49-13
			CompuServe: 100015.3123@compuserve.com

STAR MINES

by Jari Karjala

Unlike the other shooter games in this collection, which owe their ancestry to Space Invaders, Star Mines (Figure 14-2) is more reminiscent of a game called Asteroids, in which you have to blast away at large flying mountains until you break them into small flying mountains.

In Star Mines, however, you must guide your spaceship through a series of brightly colored mazes, collecting bonusoids and avoiding star mines of all kinds. The game doesn't quite obey Newton's laws of physics. There's just enough friction to slow your ship down to a stop whenever you stop accelerating, and you can bounce off the walls without any damage too.

Star Mines has simple but effective graphics. The game also supports the Sound Blaster card. The nice thing about Star Mines is that you can play the game fast and furious, or you can play it slow and calculating. It's up to you.

Figure 14-2
STAR MINES
It takes real skill to play Bumper Cars in space.

Directory: \CHAP14\STARMINE
To Play: **SM2.EXE**
Date: 9-1-93
Archive: SMINES.ZIP
Registration: No money. Send a postcard.

Contact: Jari Karjala
Veropellontie 11
00740 Helsinki
Finland

PATRIOT COMMAND

by John E. Stenersen

There used to be a game in the arcades called Missile Command in which nuclear missiles were coming down on your cities, and you had to stop them with antiballistic missiles. It was a very frustrating game, because every time you missed, a city disappeared. When you had no more cities, you were out of the game.

Patriot Command, version 1.3, (Figure 14-3) plays much the same as Missile Command, but the scale of mayhem has been significantly reduced. This time, you're using Patriot missiles to defend your installations against incoming SCUDS. The simulated SCUDS are much more accurate than their real-life counterparts, but that's to make the game interesting. Once you get some skill with this game, it becomes a very cathartic exercise to blow up the incoming weapons — especially if you pretend they're really subpoenas fired by rabid lawyers.

Directory: \CHAP14\PATRIOT
To Play: **PATDEMO.EXE**
Date: 11-9-93
Archive: PATRIOT.ZIP
Registration: $20

Contact: Timber Valley Software
Ordering Department
P.O. Box 80301
Portland, OR 97280-1301

Figure 14-3
PATRIOT COMMAND
Stop the missiles, before the missiles stop you.

INVASION OF THE MUTANT SPACE BATS OF DOOM

by Mike Pooler

artwork by Dave Cockerill

This game probably has the most understated title of any shooter game we've encountered. Never mind that. The game is also one of the most fun. The mutant space bats travel in flocks (herds?) and they can be pretty ferocious opponents. They swoop around the screen like no other enemies, and they can be very difficult to destroy.

As expected, your goal is to destroy as many space bats as you can. You'll have to use evasive maneuvers to avoid them and their weapons, but when you hit a bat, its power crystal pops out. If you grab it, you get the power. If you're good enough, you can get through all 21 rounds and you can start over again. In the registered version, there are 64 rounds and an animated sequence if you win the game.

There are different kinds of power crystals. Each one improves your ship a different way. When you catch a crystal, your ship sparkles and the window on the left of the screen tells you its effect. There are also bonuses to be won off the bonus board, so it helps to watch that too.

The animation is terrific (see Figure 14-4). The effect when your ship gets blown up is very nice; not quite enough to overcome the annoyance of being blown up, but at least you're going out in style.

Directory:	\CHAP14\SPACEBAT
To Play:	**BATS.EXE**
Date:	7-31-94
Archive:	BATS25.ZIP
Registration:	$15 + $3 shipping and handling

Contact: Pop Software
P.O. Box 60995
Sunnyvale, CA 94088

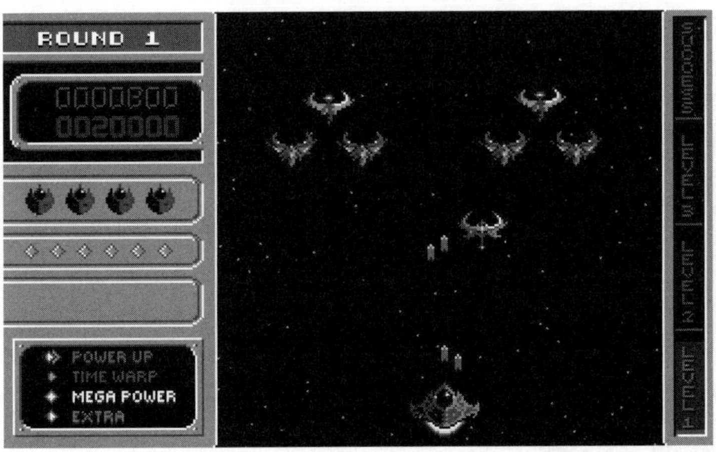

Figure 14-4
INVASION OF THE MUTANT SPACE BATS OF DOOM
Did you ever have one of those days when *nothing* went right?

ZONE 66

by Tomasz Pytel

graphics by Joe Hitchens

music by Kenny Chow

Zone 66 is spectacular! It has some of the most wonderful imagery and animation we've ever seen in an action game. Unlike all of the other shooter games in this collection, Zone 66 allows you to fly in any direction: up, down, sideways, diagonally — the playing field scrolls smoothly beneath you.

Your job is to bomb enemy installations and shoot down hostile planes. But watch out for ground fire. It can be deadly. The game lets you inflict massive damage on the local terrain, but you have to watch your resources. Periodically, you must return to base to reload fuel, missiles, and bombs. It's very challenging to play.

Zone 66 (see Figure 14-5) is an *extremely* high-intensity, fast-action, state-of-the-art shoot-em-up. It requires a 386 machine or better, and it might not run if you have any TSR (terminate-and-stay-resident) programs stored in memory, so you'll probably have to reboot with a clean configuration. The ZONE66.DOC file will help you get the program running. A boot disk is recommended.

It's definitely worth the effort, because this is as good a shooter game as has ever been written for the PC. Zone 66 is simply stunning, both in its graphics and its music and sound effects. This is one of the best games in this collection.

Directory: \CHAP14\ZONE66
To Play: **ZONE66.EXE**
Date: 9-22-93
Archive: ZONE66.ZIP
Registration: $34 (for episodes 1-4, includes shipping)
$49 (for episodes 1-8, includes shipping)

Contact: Epic MegaGames
10406 Holbrook Drive
Potomac, MD 20854
Tel: 301-299-3841
Tel: 800-972-7434 (orders only)
Fax: 301-299-3841

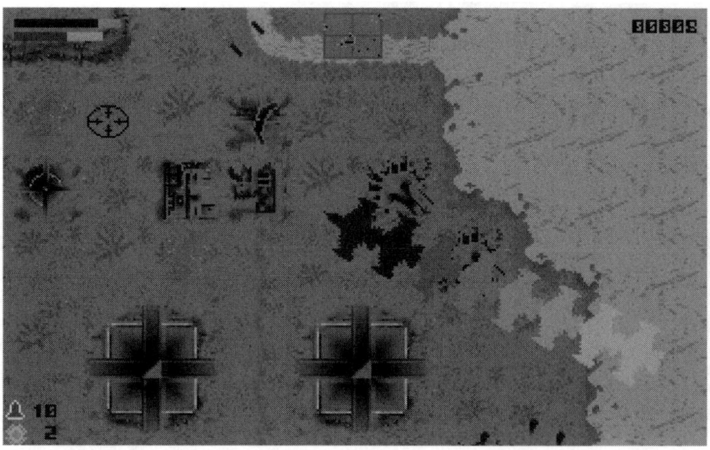

Figure 14-5
ZONE 66
Turn on your cloaking device and smoke the enemy.

RAPTOR

programming by Scott Host

artwork by Rich Fleider, Tim Neveu

level design by Jim Molinets

sound by Paul Radek

music by Matt Murphy

Wow! And double wow! Apogee has done it again. They've redefined the standard of excellence for a whole category. Shooter games will never be the same again. Raptor has arrived.

Raptor (Figure 14-6) is a very fast, action game, incredibly intense, extremely challenging. The sound effects are overwhelming, the music is driving and powerful, and the graphics — well, the graphics are simply the best you're ever going to see in a shooter game. They're so realistic, they're cinematic. It's like playing a movie.

The registered version has three separate adventures, which will take you to even more stunning battlefields: the red deserts of Mars, the jungles of India, the dark side of the Moon, an erupting volcano, and other wastelands of the world.

As with other state-of-the-art games, Raptor requires a 386 machine or better. A sound card isn't required, but it will add new meaning to the word *impact*.

Directory:	\CHAP14\RAPTOR
Run:	**RAP.EXE**
Date:	4-1-94
Source:	RAPTOR.ZIP
Registration:	$40 (for all three episodes, includes shipping) (See ORDER.DOC for combo pack pricing.)

Contact: Apogee Software
P.O. Box 496389
Garland, TX 75049
Tel: 800-GAME-123

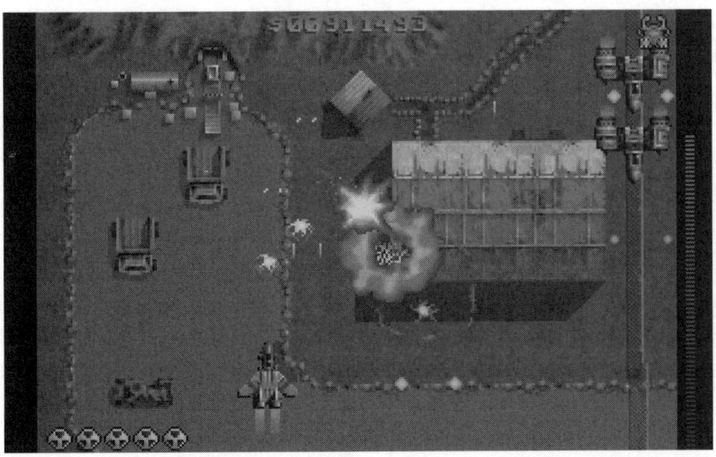

Figure 14-6
RAPTOR
Turn down the lights. Turn up the sound. Listen to the house shake. Listen to your neighbors scream. Break your lease. Meet your local police. Have fun.

Shh. Here's a hint on how to access the *secret mode* in Raptor.

At the bottom of the mission-selection screen is a rocker switch. Click on that. Then click the first and third buttons to the right of the rocker switch. Then select your mission. In the shareware version, you can only select the Bravo Mission, and in addition to all the usual enemies, you'll also get to fight monkeys, lizards, and cows… .

CHAPTER 15

FIGHTERS

FIGHTERS

The issue of violence in video games is a sensitive one. Do these games create unhealthy role models for impressionable adolescents, as some critics claim? Or do they provide a healthy outlet for aggression, as defenders would have us believe. There are valid points to be made on both sides of this discussion.

Many people find the sight of two human beings slugging away at each other repugnant; turning it into a video game fantasy does not lessen the violence. If anything, by allowing us to become desensitized to it, it may provide the opposite effect. On the other hand, most game players are more than capable of distinguishing between fantasy violence and real life. Some critics say that it is not simply a matter of role models, it is a matter of the way of thinking that these games engender — that problems can be solved through aggressive means. The issue is likely to remain unresolved.

One thing is for certain, personal combat games have become one of the most popular segments of video arcade gaming. The animation in games like Street Fighter II and Mortal Kombat II is slick and impressive, giving a sense of considerable control and power to the player. Many players approach the games as contests of gaming skill, not as acts of aggression. And this provides considerable evidence that the defenders have a valid point. Here is a nonviolent way for an individual to sublimate aggressive tendencies.

There is another issue to consider — is it the violence that some people object to? Or the *depiction* of violence?

Consider the difference between Pac Man and Wolfenstein 3D. The games are topologically identical. You run through a maze looking for treasure and trying to evade and destroy enemies. Most people think Pac Man is cute. Most people react with a mixture of dismay and fascination the first time they are exposed to the graphic mayhem in Wolfenstein and Doom. Yet Wolfenstein and Doom have both proven themselves far more popular on the home computer than all of the implementations of Pac Man. One has to wonder, would Pac Man be more attractive if the ghosts were armed with chain saws or if Pac Man had a rocket launcher?

Apparently, we as a species have a morbid fascination with violence. Do the games prepare us for the violence of life, or do they create a context in which violence is inevitable? These are troubling questions, and to those of us who love computer games, they are inescapable questions, because if we should take the stand that violence is abhorrent in games like Mortal Kombat, then isn't it also abhorrent to throw an axe to kill a dwarf in Adventure? Isn't it also abhorrent to use a wand of fire to zap an orc in Nethack? The only difference is the detail of the graphics, right? Where should we draw the line? I don't have an answer to any of these questions. I do know that it is important that we ask them. And it is even more important that we provide an appropriate context for the games that we play and that we allow our children to play. Whether we allow the violent ones or not, the real issue is personal responsibility.

We found several fighting games in the shareware distribution channels, including one commercial demo. We had some problems running almost all of them. We found only one that we felt should be included in this collection.

(As we prepared to go to press, we were told that Epic MegaGames is preparing a spectacular fighter game called One Must Fall. If it's as good as all the other Epic offerings, it will be well worth watching for.)

SANGO FIGHTER

by Panda Entertainment Tech. Co., Ltd.

Sango, also called Sango Fighter, is set in the twilight years of the Han Dynasty in medieval China. Although it has little to do with the game, the documentation includes a brief history of how the Han dynasty weakened itself by passing too much authority to the warlords. Inevitably, the warlords began fighting among themselves. Eventually, the military genius Cao Cao became a serious threat to the other warlords, targeting Liu Bei first. The subsequent wars are the historical source for many great military traditions, including Sun Tzu's definitive book on strategy and cunning, *The Art of War*.

Not that any of this has a great deal to do with how you play the game itself, but it does show that the authors have taken the time to do their homework and strive for a sense of accuracy in their presentation. Figure 15-1 shows some of the accurate costume and sharp graphics. The effort should be acknowledged. Too many games are just a hodge-podge of scattered mythologies, some religious, some fictional, some historic. It's a pleasant surprise to find a game that tries to stay true to its source material. The introductory screens are particularly nice.

You can play against the computer, or you can play as a two-player game with both people sharing the keyboard. You can use also use the joystick. As with other games, both fighters can throw magical fire and leap over tall buildings in a single bound.

Figure 15-1
SANGO FIGHTER
What we have here is a failure to communicate.

We had some problems trying to exit the two-player game on both of our test machines; we had to reboot to exit. A boot disk may be necessary for some machines.

Directory:	\CHAP15\SANGO
To Play:	**SANGO.EXE**
Date:	8-31-93
Archive:	SANGO.ZIP
Registration:	$35 + $5 shipping

Contact: ACCEND Proj.
P.O. Box 484
Warrensburg, MO 64093
Tel: 816-429-2520

CHAPTER 16

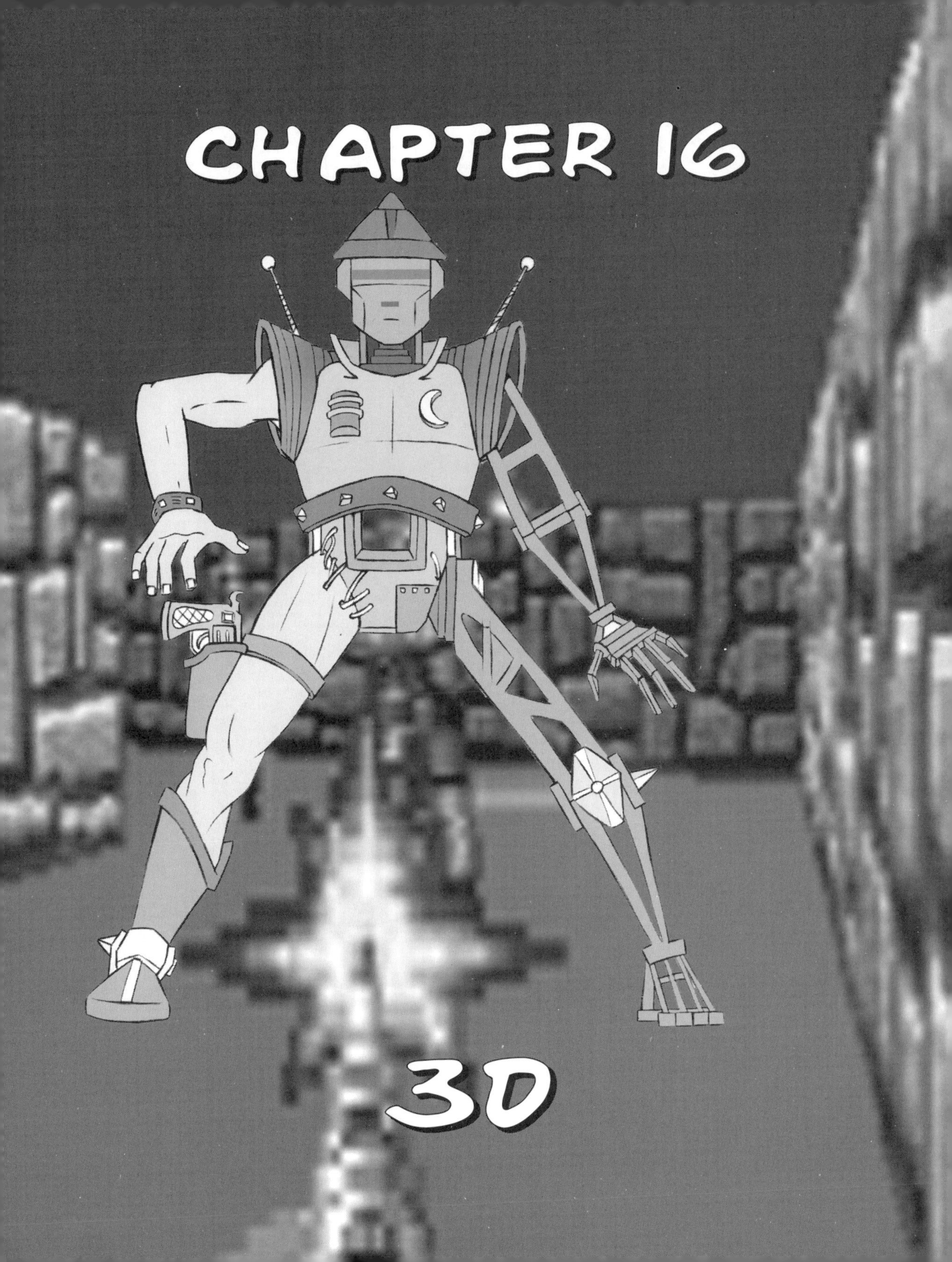

3D

3D

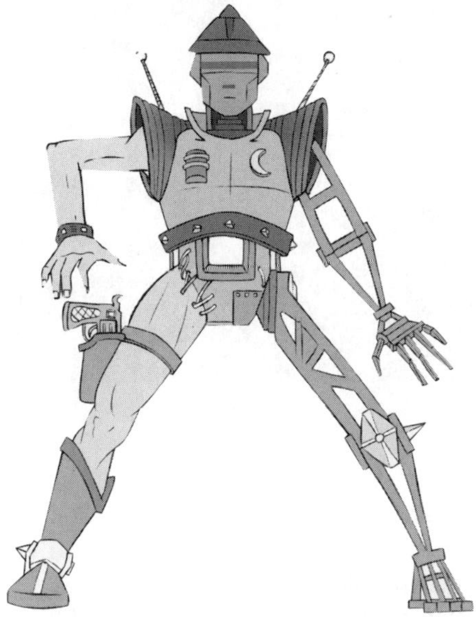

The hottest new category of gaming software is the 3D adventure. This is a point-of-view experience that puts you right into the game environment. Instead of looking at the dungeon from above, you're *inside* it. On a big screen monitor, with stereo speakers connected to your sound card, the experience can sometimes be very intense.

WOLFENSTEIN 3D

In 1991, the gaming geniuses at ID Software produced a breakthrough game called Wolfenstein 3D (Figure 16-1).

Distributed through Apogee publishing, Wolf 3D quickly became the most successful and the most talked about virtual reality game ever published for the personal computer. In Wolf 3D, you are an American agent prowling around a Nazi castle, recovering stolen treasures while eluding *and shooting* guards, officers, and super-powered Nazi leaders.

You are given a point-of-view window into the corridors and chambers of the castle. Using the arrow keys, mouse, or joystick, you explore each level's maze of traps and torture chambers. You must find caches of food and ammunition to replenish yourself as you go. The game has its own unique style, and despite the gruesome subject matter, there are even moments of bizarre humor. When you kill one of the big bosses, for instance, he keels over calling plaintively (in German) for his mommy.

Wolf 3D is a virtual reality variant of Pac Man, but with a lot more gore. It's a point-of-view maze where you gobble treasures while desperately avoiding monsters. This

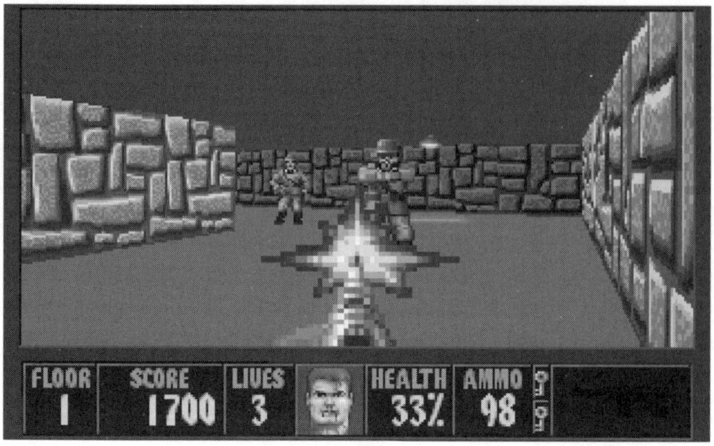

Figure 16-1
WOLF 3D
This is not how to win friends, but it is how you win at Wolfenstein.

particular realization has not escaped the authors either. (If you've played the registered game, you know what I mean.)

Wolfenstein generates its graphic views in real time, so you can turn, advance, back up, and shoot as if you are actually there. The sound effects attached to various events lend a compelling air of realism too. (You'll need a Sound Blaster or compatible card for the full effect.) On slower machines, the movement is jerky, so you have to reduce the size of the view window to regain smooth movement.

The game has four levels of difficulty, from "Can I Play Daddy?" to "Death Incarnate." If you're playing on the Death Incarnate level, you're likely to find that there are a lot more guards roaming around the halls and they're a lot better armed. You're likely to spend as much time dying as killing. If running up a high score isn't important, here's a useful hint. Hold down the I-L-M keys all at the same time and your health and ammunition and weaponry will all be set to maximum values. You'll find the chain gun is quite an effective weapon.

Now that all of that has been said, I do want to express some serious concern about the subject matter. Many of us lost loved ones to the Nazi madness, either on the battlefield or in the death camps. So it isn't out of order to consider whether or not this game is in bad taste. I'm not the only one who has had second thoughts about this. The GAMERS forum on CompuServe has seen many spirited discussions on this very subject.

It isn't simply the vivid representation of killing other human beings that worries some; it's the Nazi-like mentality. *In this game, to defeat the enemy, you have to act like him.* And it is the brutal actions of the Nazis that we find so appalling. Convincing ourselves that we're the good guys, therefore it's all right to shoot the bad guys isn't a very good argument. Nobody ever thinks of himself as the bad guy. Parents who object to war toys will probably object to this game as well. This is *definitely* not a game for young or impressionable players. Some people think it might not even be suitable for its target audience, adolescent males.

Others have argued, just as credibly, that as long as a player is able to differentiate between reality and fantasy, the game is mostly harmless. And, to its credit, Wolf 3D has produced some awareness of the Nazi atrocities in World War II for many people who might otherwise never have considered the matter. The game provided me with several opportunities to begin telling my own son about the horrors of World War II; so even though Wolf 3D is not exactly great history, it does open a useful doorway to discussion. And it does help keep some very important memories alive.

Most gamers, however, are going to come to Wolf 3D for its intense action. Any consideration of philosophy or morality will probably be swamped by an adrenaline rush of excitement. Whatever else you think about Wolfenstein's subject matter, it is undeniably one of the most playable and successful games ever designed for the desktop computer.

Directory:	CHAP16\WOLF3D	Contact:	Apogee Software
To Play:	**WOLF3D.EXE**		P.O. Box 496389
Date:	1-1-93		Garland, TX 75049
Archive:	WOLF3D.ZIP		Tel: 800-GAME-123
Registration:	$49.95 (for all six episodes)		
	$10 (for hint book)		

A commercial version of Wolfenstein 3D, called Spear of Destiny is also available. Spear of Destiny can be ordered from Apogee or purchased in most software stores. It has 18 levels and two secret levels — and a breathtaking finale. If you enjoy Wolfenstein, be sure to check out Spear of Destiny.

Wolfenstein Add-Ons

Wolf 3D has become one of the most spectacularly successful games in computer history; so much so that it has even inspired a whole cottage industry of mappers and editors and new episodes. There are utilities available (written by Wolf 3D enthusiasts, definitely *not* provided by Apogee or ID) for changing the scenery, the animated characters, the sounds, and even the floor layout of the various levels of the game.

Every aspect of the Wolfenstein environment has been disassembled by devoted fans, and it is now possible to design a whole new game around the Wolfenstein graphics engine. And some dedicated (obsessive) fans have done just that, much to Apogee's dismay. Most of these graphic redesigns are interesting stunts — good for a few minutes worth of amusement, but not particularly playable in the long run. In one particularly bizarre tweak, you can even hunt down and kill Barney the Dinosaur. This is a joke that's probably funnier to think about than to actually see.

However, I do want to a acknowledge that enthusiastic (obsessive) Wolfenstein fans have also created *hundreds* of new add-on levels for the original game. Indeed, some of the ones I've seen have been quite well done; several are very challenging. Collections of these new episodes can often be found on computer bulletin boards or at computer swap meets.

Most of the amateur levels will work only with the registered version of Wolfenstein, so you will have to purchase the full game from Apogee to play them, but some caution is advised here. You cannot depend on amateur episodes being totally bug-free. This is because there are limits to what the game engine is capable of, and many of the amateur designers do not know what those limits are. Some of these episodes break the rules of good Wolfenstein design, and they may hang up your computer or produce other weird behaviors.

Because of that, we have not included in this collection any of the Wolfenstein map editors or any of the amateur levels available. We are, however, including an excellent map-making utility, which will help you find your way through some of the tougher levels.

WolfMap

by David Lummis

Wolfmap is a very easy utility to use. Simply copy WOLFMAP.EXE into your Wolfenstein directory and type **WOLFMAP** and press ENTER. The program will ask you which level of the game you want to map, or if you want to map all ten levels.

You type in a number, the program reads the data files for the game and writes the map to your disk. The file extension identifies the level. If you map level three, for instance, the resultant file will be WMAP.L03. Because the map files are ASCII-standard, you can print them to almost any printer.

Wolfmap, seen in Figure 16-2, is compatible with all six episodes of the registered Wolfenstein. It will also work with the shareware game. Read WOLFMAP.DOC for further details. (Please note: this game mapper is not a product of Apogee.)

Directory: \CHAP16\WOLF3D\WOLFMAP
To Start: **WOLFMAP.EXE**
Date: 8-12-92
Archive: WOLFMP.ZIP

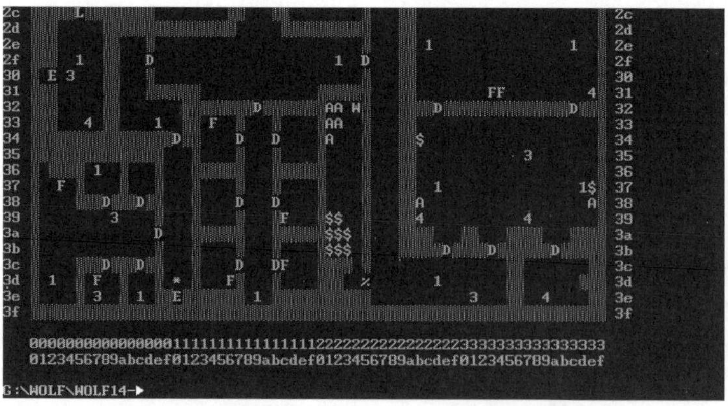

Figure 16-2
WOLFMAP
A Wolf 3D mapping utility.

Wolf FAQ

by Stanley Stasiak

W3D-330.FAQ is release 3.30 of the Wolf 3D Frequently Asked Questions file. It is the most up-to-date and comprehensive collection of Wolfenstein information that you are likely to find anywhere.

Stanley Stasiak, the author of this file, is obviously the number one fan of Wolf 3D. This is everything you ever wanted to know, and probably quite a bit more.

Here are all the hints you need to play the game, information about how the various features of it work, all the known cheats, and even a revealing peek under the hood. This is one of the most fascinating background documents you will ever see about any game. The file even includes a listing of Wolfenstein utilities and add-ons that enthusiastic (obsessive) fans have created for the game.

Please be aware, this file is not a product of either ID or Apogee.

Directory:	CHAP16\WOLF3D\FAQ
To View:	**TYPE W3D.330.FAQ ¦ MORE**
Date:	2-22-94
Archive:	WOLFAQ.ZIP

ETERNAM

by Intracorp, Inc.

Eternam is not like any other 3D game in this collection. Created by the makers of the popular Alone In The Dark game, Eternam (Figure 16-3) is a well-implemented, humorous adventure with great sound and graphics. Well, graphics anyway. If you want to hear the sound, you've gotta register the game. But, considering the quality of the rest of the game, we have no doubt that the sound is of the highest quality.

Figure 16-3
ETERNAM
This is a virtually real world.

In Eternam, you are a rowdy rapscallion, trying to rescue the Duke's beloved son, who has been most heinously kidnapped. But before you can set out on your quest, you must prove your worthiness and skill in a series of tests set up by the Duke and his henchmen. None of the best knights in the region can do it. Could it be that only a worthless wanderer like you can complete the Duke's tasks and set out to rescue his heir? Doubtful. Very doubtful. However, the Duke is willing to give you a chance, and I'm not one to argue with such a powerful person as the Duke.

Eternam is unique in that it provides two different perspectives. When you are wandering through the wilderness, you are in virtual reality mode, with a 3D view of the world around you. You can even use the F1 and F2 keys to change the angle of the view. While this may or may not help you win the game, you CAN do it. On the other hand, when you are in a building, you have the familiar video game view — you watch your character move as you guide him through his adventure.

And what an adventure it is! You must interact with the various creatures and people of the realm. Make sure you talk to everybody. Some of your conversations will be hilarious, others deadly serious. Many will provide clues to help you on your quest. Also, as with any adventure game, examine everything and take whatever you can get your filthy paws on. Few things are in an adventure by chance, so anything you find might be useful somewhere in your adventure. Most of all, have fun in this most enjoyable of fatal distractions.

Directory: \CHAP16\ETERNAM
To Play: **ETERNAM.BAT**
Date: 4-16-93
Archive: ETERNAM.ZIP
Registration: $49.95 (Includes full version of Eternam, with sound and additional islands.)

Contact: Intracorp, Inc.
7200 NW 19th Street
Suite #500
Miami, FL 33126
Tel: 800-468-7226
FL Residents: 305-591-5900

Note: As this book goes to press, Intracorp, Inc. plans to replace Eternam in its lineup with newer games. Consequently, you may have difficulty obtaining this game, but, maybe — if enough people like Eternam and let 'em know — they might keep this excellent adventure available.

BLAKE STONE – ALIENS OF GOLD

by JAM

The Wolfenstein graphics engine has been licensed by JAM for Apogee's newest game, Blake Stone — Aliens of Gold. It is recognizably the same game engine, but it has been very nicely enhanced. This time, it's a science fiction theme, with aliens, robots, and the inevitable mad scientist.

Blake Stone (see Figure 16-4) has a much wider variety of villains and monsters to battle, a larger library of weapons, and a greater vocabulary of sounds. In addition, it also provides an auto-mapping feature, and textured floors and ceilings. If the game movements are too slow or jerky, you can reduce the size of the screen, or you can

Figure 16-4
BLAKE STONE
Beware of the stobor.

turn off the floor and/or ceiling textures. This is a very thoughtful feature. These are state-of-the-art graphics, but the authors obviously understand that not everybody will be playing the game on a state-of-the-art machine.

As a game, Blake Stone provides the same kinds of puzzles as Wolfenstein: explore the level, find the secret passages, pick up ammunition and health, kill the villains, recover the treasures, get the keys, and so on. Virtual Pac Man again. But thankfully, it's nowhere near as viscerally intense.

Blake Stone is a much less *serious* game than Wolf 3D. It's a different experience, exciting without being relentlessly gory. The game environment is bright and futuristic, the creatures roaming the halls look more like comic book escapees than nightmares, and you have a much wider choice of weapons to use. Indeed, the weaponry in Blake Stone is very impressive. So if you have reservations about Wolf 3D's theme or Catacomb Abyss, you will probably find Blake Stone much more to your liking.

There's a lot to do and discover here and there are a lot of nice surprises. You can start this game thinking you're just fooling around, but in a very short time, you may become totally hooked.

Directory: \CHAP16\BLAKE
To Play: **BS_AOG.EXE**
Date: 2-11-94
Archive: BSTONE.ZIP
BBS Archive: \CHAP16\BLAKE\BBS
Registration: $59.95 (for all three episodes)

Contact: Apogee Software
P.O. Box 496389
Garland, TX 75049
Tel: 800-GAME-123

Hints

As a bonus, we've included BSJOURN.TXT, the unofficial journal of Blake Stone, a hint file that should help you considerably as you work your way through the game. Also provided is BLAKE.TXT, a list of parameters and cheat keys. Both text files are in the \CHAP16\BLAKE\HINTS subdirectory.

Directory: \CHAP16\BLAKE\HINTS
To View: **TYPE BLAKE.TXT ¦ MORE** (for BLAKE.TXT)
TYPE BSJOURN.TXT ¦ MORE (for the Blake Stone journal)
Archive: BSCHEAT.ZIP (BLAKE.TXT)
BSJRN.ZIP (BSJOURN.TXT)

Mapping Utility

We've also included BLAKEMAP.EXE, a utility program that will let you generate maps of each level of Blake Stone, whether you're playing the shareware or registered game. This is found in \CHAP16\BLAKE\MAPS.

To activate any of the cheat modes, you must start the game with the command BS_AOG POWERBALL. Then, when you see the JAM logo screen, press both the left-SHIFT and the right-SHIFT and hold them until you see the PG-13 rating screen. You should hear a distinctive "ching" sound to let you know that you have activated the cheat modes. It can be a little tricky, but once you get it working, you can enter the various cheat keys as you play. For instance BACKSPACE-G puts you into the "god" mode, which means you can't be hurt by enemy bullets.

Ah, if only real life were this easy. . . .

Directory: \CHAP16\BLAKE\MAPS
To Run: **BLAKEMAP.EXE**
Archive: BLAKEMAP.ZIP

CHAPTER 17

DOOM

DOOM

The game is Doom. It is the single most astonishing game ever written for the personal computer. A breathtaking accomplishment, it is certain to stand as a landmark effort for years to come. Make no mistake, Doom, seen in Figure 17-1, is a breakthrough piece of work, both as a game and as a graphics programming triumph. It is going to change the face of computer gaming forever.

No player is going to be untouched by the stunning power of the adventure. No programmer is going to be unmoved by its amazing graphics engine. (The number of programmers who have already slit their wrists in despair is surpassed only by the number of those who have already died of envy.) Doom is already an extraordinary shareware hit, and it promises to become an even bigger phenomenon in the months to come.

Boot up Doom and you become a space-marine blasting your way through a series of extraterrestrial installations infested with alien demons from hell. No, this time, it's for *real.* And this time, the environment is so much richer, so much more detailed, that it's like stepping into another world. This is the very best virtual reality game of all.

If you could get Clive Barker to choreograph an H. R. Giger ballet, with libretto by H. P. Lovecraft, you could not create a more horrifying environment. Doom is a place so terrifying, even Death travels in pairs.

The imagery here is so compelling and so realistic that it is not advisable to play this game late at night when you're alone in the house. I mean it. Doom is *disturbing*. It should be R-rated. It is definitely not suitable for impressionable children. In fact, it probably isn't even suitable for any child under the age of forty.

Almost every other 3D game exists in a right-angled world, with perfectly square blocks of scenery. The graphics in other 3D games have a flat, cartoon-like quality. But Doom is not a cartoon dungeon. It is a window into a very real and very terrifying world. Here, instead of the blocky rectangular mazes that you've seen elsewhere, there are vast panoramas and frightening vistas.

Doom is a world of curved walls, angled walls, windows, and disturbingly off-center rooms. There are elevators that go up into gloomy towers and down into even gloomier dungeons. There are toxic, green slime pits that you can fall into, precarious ledges above you from which demons hurl fireballs, spiral staircases that curve around and down — and there are lava-textured floors and radiant ceilings, all at various heights. Beware the ceilings! Some of them can lower suddenly to crush you.

In some places, the walls themselves are animated. As the scenery recedes into the distance, it darkens with atmospheric gloom. Indeed, much of the mood of the game is enhanced by the gothic lighting. In some places, the lights flash on and off; in other places, the only illumination is the intermittent flash from the muzzle of your rifle.

And the creatures — my god, the creatures! There are fireball-hurling imps, horrendous demons, and barons of Hell so huge and terrifying that the first time I saw one, I leapt backward out of my chair with an involuntary yelp loud enough to scare everyone in the house. There are mutant humans, flaming skulls, loathesome caecodemons, and a couple of monstrous things better left unmentioned.

Thankfully, Doom gives you a terrific choice of weapons — a shotgun, a chain gun, a rocket launcher, a plasma rifle, and even the legendary BFG-9000. (BFG stands for Big Fun Gun, or something like that.) You can also use a chainsaw to carve up your assailants, or if you want, you can find a berserker pack and splatter the monsters with one punch of your fist. If this sounds too intense, don't panic; you can lower the violence of the game. *Or raise it.* Nightmare level is recommended for experienced Doomers only.

If this were a movie, the art direction would walk off with an Oscar. And so would the creepy sound effects. Some of the monster-roars are so disturbing that I won't play with earphones on. And I won't play alone late at night either. After a day or two of playing Doom, I realized I was afraid to go around corners or enter unfamiliar rooms.

NETWORK DOOM

Doom also provides for network play. You can play over a modem, a null-modem cable, or a local area network. Up to four people at a time can bludgeon their way through the nightmare world of Doom. You can play cooperatively, or you can play in death-match mode — which is exactly what it sounds like: every man for himself, and the last one standing wins.

There's a certain irony to this. Twenty years after the first point-of-view, network maze game was demonstrated on the big machines at the M.I.T. computer labs, it's finally come home to the personal computer — with a vengeance. Played in death-match mode, Doom starts each player out at a different place in the maze, and each has access to fresh supplies. It is immediately obvious that considerable thought has been given to the playability of every situation.

But you're going to need a fast machine. I recommend a 486 with a fast video card, preferably local bus. Anything less than that may be insufficient; you'll have to reduce the size of the playing screen to keep the movement smooth. Even a state-of-the-art

Figure 17-1
DOOM

machine is going to be stressed by the amount of calculation involved in updating the graphics in Doom. You can almost hear your CPU sigh in relief when you exit the game.

If you have too much money in your wallet, you can also set up Doom to run on three side-by-side screens simultaneously to give yourself a panoramic view, like an old-fashioned Cinerama movie. All you need are three identical computers, three identical monitors, and three network cards to connect them all. Properly installed, you can have your own personal nightmare. This is not recommended for people with nervous conditions or weak hearts.

FULL CIRCLE

With Doom, we have finally come full circle in our quest for the ultimate Fatal Distraction. Doom contains aspects of almost every other kind of game discussed in this book. There is a large explorable environment. There are risks and rewards. There are tools, weapons, and bonuses. There are mazes and barriers and secret passages. There are challenging puzzles, complicated by deadly crossfire. There are dangers here of all kinds, including a variety of monsters that defy description. Each level is harder than the last, and there are surprises at the end that will scare the yell out of you. Doom is an awesome achievement.

A commercial version, Doom II – Hell on Earth, is scheduled for release before the end of 1994. It will have stunning new features, and terrifying new creatures, and I can't say more than that. Watch for it though. It should be spectacular.

Directory:	\CHAP17\DOOM
To Play:	**DOOM.EXE**
Date:	2-17-94
Archive:	DOOM.ZIP (ready to run)
BBS Archive:	\CHAP17\DOOM\BBS
Registration:	$45 (for all three episodes, includes shipping)

Contact: ID Software
c/o StarPak
P.O. Box 1230
Greeley, CO 80632
Tel: 800-IDGAMES
(800-434-2637)

Doom FAQ

by Hank Leukart

The single, most thorough source of information about Doom is Hank Leukart's regularly updated FAQ file. Everything you want to know about Doom can be found within.

Here are all the hints you need to play the game, information about how the various features of it work, all the known cheats, and even some fascinating background information. This is an impressive piece of documentation.

Because Doom is still under active development, Leukart will probably be updating the FAQ file to keep up with changes. The file includes information on where to find future releases, as well as a thorough discussion of all known add-ons and utilities.

Please be aware, this file is not a product of ID, but the programmers at ID acknowledge that they occasionally use it themselves to check details of their own product. Higher praise than that you cannot get.

Directory:	\CHAP17\DOOM\DOOMFAQ	Contact:	Hank Leukart
To View:	**TYPE DOOM56.FAQ : MORE**		7255 Valley View Rd.
Date:	4-19-94		Hudson, OH 44236
Archive:	DMFAQ56.ZIP	Internet:	ap641@cleveland.freenet.edu

LEVEL 2: ALIEN DOOM

by Mike Dickson, Dan Goldwasser, Marc Gordon, Bernd Kreimeier, David Lobser, and Dave Matteson

Just before this book was shipped to the printer, we learned of an absolutely incredible add-on for the registered version of Doom. This is a patch that modifies the game so that the environment comes right out of the *Alien* series of movies. Using redesigned weapons, you'll face down hideous xenomorphs right there in the Dalstrom Institute, and listen to the bone chilling clarity of the beasts' final curses and screams.

Version 1.0 is included on the CD in the BONUS directory. It's also come to our attention that the authors are now updating this remarkable add-on. By the time this book comes out, the next version may already be available. The authors report that the main place to get the newest version is via internet at the anonymous FTP site infant2.sphs.indiana.edu, but it may also be available elsewhere.

Parents should be advised that some of the language in this module is rather harsh. This addition should probably also be avoided by people with heart conditions and pregnant women.

APPENDIX A

ADVENTURE GAME TOOLKIT

Those who like adventuring really like adventuring. The evidence of this is the Adventure Game Toolkit (see Figure A-1) from Softworks. When you can't find the adventure game you most want to play, you have to write it yourself. But first you need a game engine. The AGT is generally regarded as the best adventure game engine available anywhere.

Some very talented writers have used the toolkit to create a wonderful body of work that is imaginative, innovative, and surprising. What's most impressive, as you will shortly see, is the wide range of their imaginations.

The Adventure Game Toolkit (AGT) began life as a program by Mark Welch called the Generic Adventure Game System (GAGS). Using GAGS, it was possible for the nonprogrammer to develop complete adventure games using a fixed (but relatively large) vocabulary of action verbs. David Malmberg took GAGS and made a number of enhancements including the ability to customize the vocabulary and to program complex conditional tests.

Two versions of the toolkit are available: the regular toolkit (found in \APPNDXA\TOOLKIT) and the Master's Edition (which is located in \APPNDXA\MASTERS). Shortly before we went to press, both editions were converted from shareware to freeware. This means that you may use the programs freely and distribute them freely. The registration fee is no longer required, but Dave Malmberg retains the copyright on both of the toolkits. (To avoid confusion, we've removed the order form files from the Adventure Game Toolkit.) Support for the Adventure Game Toolkits is no

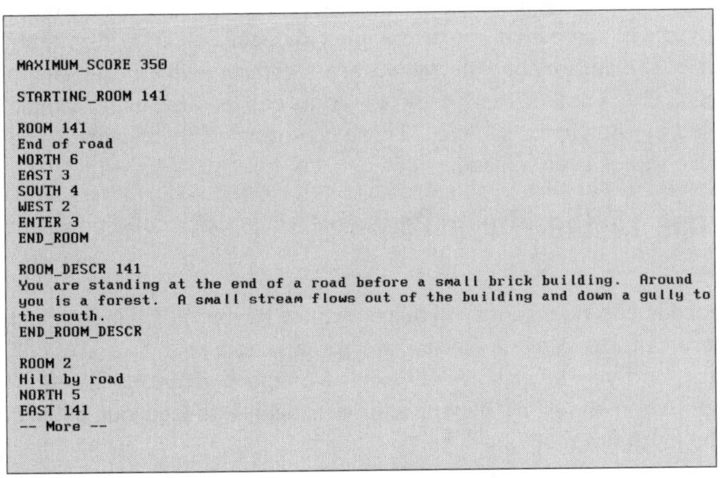

```
MAXIMUM_SCORE 350

STARTING_ROOM 141

ROOM 141
End of road
NORTH 6
EAST 3
SOUTH 4
WEST 2
ENTER 3
END_ROOM

ROOM_DESCR 141
You are standing at the end of a road before a small brick building.  Around
you is a forest.  A small stream flows out of the building and down a gully to
the south.
END_ROOM_DESCR

ROOM 2
Hill by road
NORTH 5
EAST 141
-- More --
```

Figure A-1
ADVENTURE GAME TOOLKIT
Design your own adventure.

POPHINT

Many of the games written with the Adventure Game Toolkit also come with hint files, especially written for the on-line POPHINT utility. To find out if a game has a hint file, look for a file in the same directory that has an .HNT extension. For instance, if the game is called THIEF, you want to look for a file named THIEF.HNT.

To use the hint file, type **POPHINT "FILENAME"** before you run the game. If the game is THIEF, type **POPHINT THIEF**. This will load the POPHINT utility. Then run the game as you normally do.

During the game, if you need a hint, press ALT-H and a hint box will appear onscreen. (ALT-H means hold the ALT key and the H down at the same time.) Press ESC to return to the game.

After playing the game, type **POPHINT** U to unload the POPHINT utility from the computer's memory. You must reload POPHINT separately for different adventures.

longer available from Softworks, but you may be able to get your questions answered on the CompuServe GAMERS forum.

The "Classic Edition" of the toolkit comes with several short sample games that can be studied and modified; it also comes with the complete source code for the original Colossal Cave Adventure, so you can even modify that if you want.

The "Master's Edition" contains all the features and capabilities of the classic edition plus a whole lot more. It's totally compatible with the classic edition and games originally developed for the classic edition can be easily converted. The Master's Edition allows you to create games that are approximately twice as large as those possible using the classic edition. Plus, your games can have optional graphic illustrations, sound effects, music, pop-up hints, unique fonts (EGA or VGA screens only), and a customizeable look-and-feel user interface including a menu-driven player input option. Be aware though, the Master's Edition is somewhat more complex to use, requiring a greater commitment on the part of the author; but the results are worth it. As with the classic edition of the Adventure Game Toolkit, the Master's Edition comes with many sample games. But don't be fooled by the word "sample." These are some of the cleverest and most challenging adventure games ever written.

CLIFF DIVER: Crime to the Ninth Power

by Pat Farley

If you love the classic forties film-noir genre, if you're a fan of Raymond Chandler, and if you never miss a rerun of *The Maltese Falcon*, this game is for you. You are Cliff Diver, Private Investigator, and you must solve the secret of the mysterious Zamboni Building in San Francisco. When the game begins, you have been knocked out by two thugs. You awaken on the ninth floor of ....

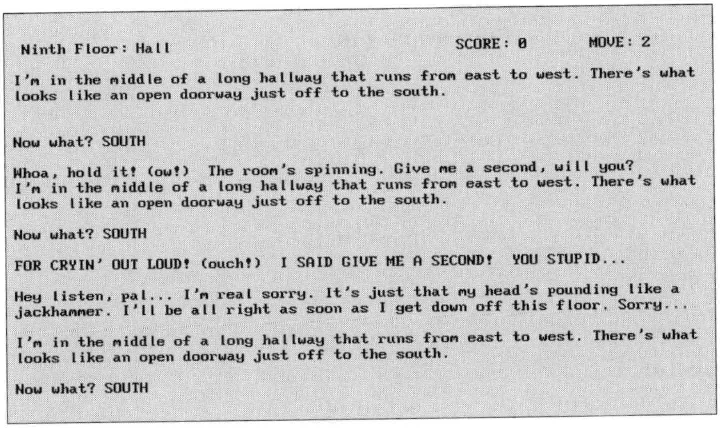

Figure A-2
CLIFF DIVER
Don't get drunk the night before you play.

Cliff Diver, shown in Figure A-2, is the 1990 winner of the Adventure Game Toolkit contest. Author Farley has brought a savage sense of fun to the work, and the text is written in the style of a pulp thriller. Even though there are parts of the environment that are not essential to the game, they're well worth exploring, just to read Cliff Diver's reactions. Stumbling into the lady's bathroom, for example. . . .

Be sure you find the flashlight before the lights go out.

Directory:	\APPNDXA\CLIFF1
To Play:	**CLIFF.BAT**
Date:	6-10-88
Archive:	CLIFF1.ZIP
Registration:	$10

Contact: Patrick Farley
1751 13th Street
Los Osos, CA. 93402
ATTN: Cliff Diver

If you get stuck, there's a hint file, CDHINTS.HNT, for use with POPHINT.EXE; and a walk-through solution file, CLIFF1.WLK.

COSMOSERVE: An Adventure Game for the BBS Enslaved

by Judith Pintar

Cosmoserve (Figure A-3) is one of the most imaginative adventure games I've ever seen. It's also one of the funniest. The version on our CD is an update of one of two co-winners of the 1991 Adventure Game Toolkit contest. (The other is the Multi-Dimensional Thief). Cosmoserve is a terrific demonstration of what can be done by an inspired author.

You are R. J. Wright, a self-employed computer consultant, working at home. Your kitchen is a mess. Your toilet won't stop running. And your Aunt Edna is a nag. Plus, you've promised to deliver a finished program at 9:30 tomorrow morning. You need to log onto Cosmoserve, a nationwide computer network, to find some valuable information — but you've forgotten your password. You know you wrote it down somewhere....

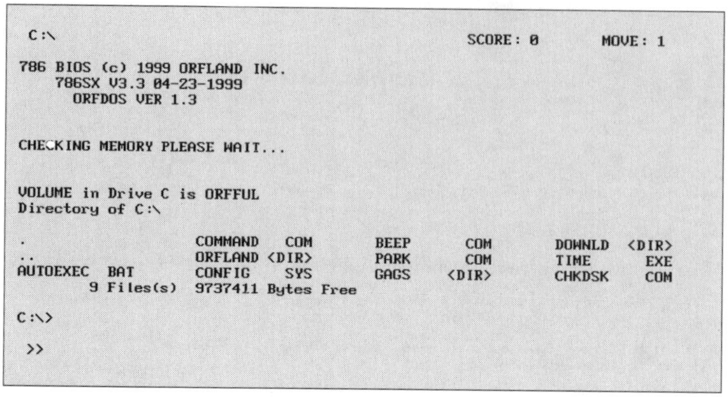

Figure A-3
COSMOSERVE.
No, this isn't DOS. This is the game!

Finding the password is the easy part. Once you are logged onto Cosmoserve, the real adventure begins. Almost the entire game is played as an on-line session; you can read files, you can play an adventure-within-an-adventure game, you can order things from the electronic mall, you can sign up for skydiving classes, explore on-line forums, and even read your e-mail. But remember, you have work to do and there are files you need to find!

Order yourself a pizza and prepare for an evening of hard work. Watch out for infectious viruses and be sure to change your password regularly.

Directory: \APPNDXA\COSMOS
To Play: **COSMOS.BAT**
Date: 7-14-94
Archive: COSMOS.ZIP
Registration: $15 and The Meaning of Life (if you know it)

Contact: Judith Pintar
P.O. Box 11728
Milwaukee, WI 53211
CompuServe 76636,2067

COSMOS.SOL, a solution file, is included in case you get stuck.

A DUDLEY DILEMMA

by Lane Barrow

Have you ever wanted to go to Harvard and search for knowledge, adventure, and a diploma? Here's your chance. A Dudley Dilemma, shown in Figure A-4, is the 1988 winner of the Adventure Game Toolkit contest.

In this game, you prowl around the Harvard campus, both aboveground and below; everywhere from Lehman Hall to the steam tunnels that heat the buildings. You will encounter your fellow students, various local inhabitants, and ultimately the dean. You must obtain a gown and cap and a tassel, if you want to graduate. To do that, you must

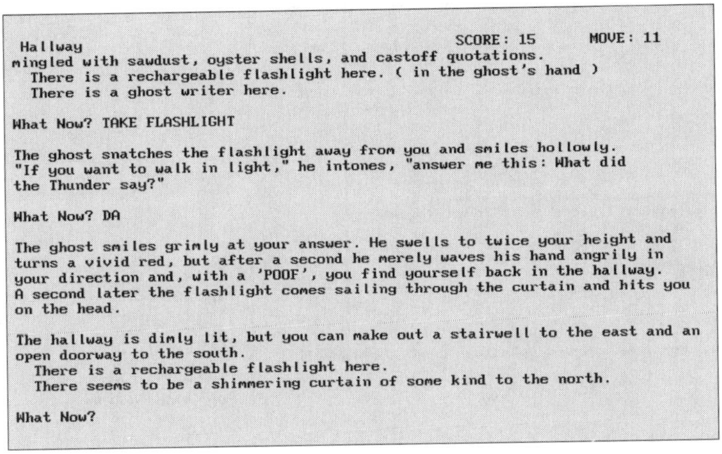

```
Hallway                                        SCORE: 15      MOVE: 11
mingled with sawdust, oyster shells, and castoff quotations.
  There is a rechargeable flashlight here. ( in the ghost's hand )
  There is a ghost writer here.

What Now? TAKE FLASHLIGHT

The ghost snatches the flashlight away from you and smiles hollowly.
"If you want to walk in light," he intones, "answer me this: What did
the Thunder say?"

What Now? DA

The ghost smiles grimly at your answer. He swells to twice your height and
turns a vivid red, but after a second he merely waves his hand angrily in
your direction and, with a 'POOF', you find yourself back in the hallway.
A second later the flashlight comes sailing through the curtain and hits you
on the head.

The hallway is dimly lit, but you can make out a stairwell to the east and an
open doorway to the south.
  There is a rechargeable flashlight here.
  There seems to be a shimmering curtain of some kind to the north.

What Now?
```

Figure A-4
DUDLEY DILEMMA
Where Yale is a four-letter word.

solve all the problems of higher education, and quite a few that have nothing to do with higher education.

I suspect that this adventure is funnier if you've actually been to Harvard; but even ordinary mortals (and Yale graduates) can still enjoy this adventure game. A Dudley Dilemma is a delightful diversion.

Directory:	\APPNDXA\DUDLEY
To Play:	**DUDLEY.BAT**
Date:	2-13-94
Archive:	DUDLEY.ZIP

If you get stuck, the solution can be found in the file DUDLEY.SOL.

THE WORLD'S HARDEST ADVENTURE

by A. Fielding with additional material by Dave Malmberg

Somewhere nearby is the old Murgatroid Mansion, where it is rumored a fortune in gold, jewels and other treasure is hidden. Many adventurers have sought the treasure, but few who entered the Mansion have ever been seen again.

In The World's Hardest Adventure (seen in Figure A-5) you start out next to a wall surrounding Murgatroid Mansion. But there is no way in. There is, however, a path that leads off to the north. If you follow this path, you are likely to find some very familiar scenery. It might help if you are familiar with the Colossal Cave and Zork. Then again, it might not. But you're definitely in for some interesting surprises.

This game really does live up to its title as the world's hardest adventure (Figure A-5). If there is a harder adventure game anywhere, I haven't found it yet. And I'm not sure I want to. I'd like to have time for a life.

WARNING: THIS IS FOR EXPERIENCED ADVENTURERS ONLY.

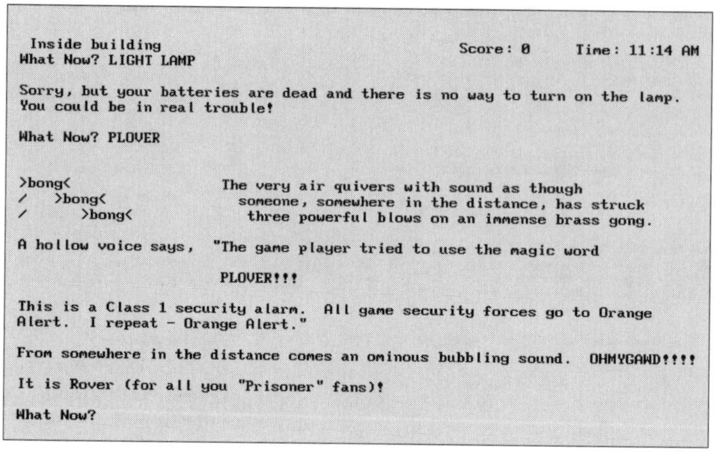

Figure A-5
THE WORLD'S HARDEST ADVENTURE.
Everything you know is wrong.

Directory:	\APPNDXA\HARDEST
To Play:	**HARDEST.BAT**
Date:	1-09-94
Archive:	HARDEST.ZIP
Registration:	$2 (gets you the solution, and helps a needy child)

Contact: AnnoyWare
194 Belgrave Ave.
London, Ont. Canada N6C 4B9

When you register, AnnoyWare provides the solution in case you get stuck. Because the money goes to help needy children, I suggest sending more than the $2 registration fee.

HURRY, HURRY, HURRY

by Dave Malmberg

A spectacular demonstration of what's possible with the Master's Edition of the Adventure Game Toolkit! Hurry, Hurry, Hurry (seen in Figure A-6) uses music, sound effects, pictures, and different fonts to enhance a mystery that takes place in a traveling circus. The game, plus source code, is part of The Master's Edition package, but we've been given special permission to include it here, and it's well worth your attention.

This time, you're the local sheriff. You and your trusty dog, Rex, are here at the circus for an afternoon of enjoyment... and just a little peacekeeping. You'll have to take the slingshot away from a familiar little boy, and you'll want to watch out for pickpockets too; but a more serious crime has been committed, and it's up to you to solve the case before the villain gets away.

This is a terrific game for parents to play with their children, and a boffo way to introduce children to the serious puzzle-solving of adventure games. (Playing adventure games is a sneaky way to get kids to learn how to type and spell correctly. It's an even better way to teach them how to think. I strongly recommend it.)

Figure A-6.
HURRY, HURRY, HURRY
No, this is not the author.

Directory: \APPNDXA\HURRY
To Play: **HURRY.BAT**
Date: 1-1-93
Archive: HURRY.ZIP, HURRYPIX.ZIP
Registration: freeware
If you get stuck, peek at the HURRY.SOL file.

Shades of Gray – An Adventure in Black and White

by Mark Baker, Steve Bauman, Liz Ellison, Mike Laskey, Judith Pintar, Cynthia Yans, and "Hercules"

Shades of Gray, seen in Figure A-7, was conceived, written, and coded by seven people: two from England, two from the East Coast, and three from the West. They have never met each other, and have never, in fact, spoken to each other on the phone, nor even corresponded by mail. The entire project was managed through e-mail from within a private CompuServe Gamer's Forum.

That said, Shades of Gray is one of the most remarkable and imaginative adventures you're ever likely to play. Part of the game is simply finding out where you are. And then you have to find out who you are. This is not just another treasure-seeking game; this is a quest for identity, a true interactive novel. It's a very large, very complex adventure that takes place in multiple realities simultaneously, and it's up to you to determine which is fantasy and which is real.

You will probably need to use the POPHINT utility to get through this, but the hints are as clever as the game. They point you in the right direction without spoiling your

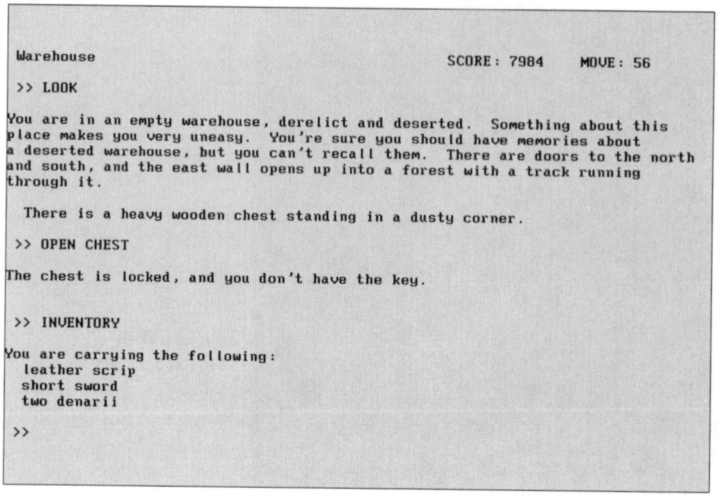

Figure A-7. SHADES OF GRAY. What is real and what is illusion?

own sense of discovery. This is the 1992 contest winner in the Special Group Effort category. The judges were unanimous in their praise.

Directory:	\APPNDXA\SOGGY
To Play:	**SOGGY.BAT**
Date:	6-05-93
Archive:	SOGGY.ZIP
Registration:	freeware

If you get stuck, there are three hint files. SOGGY.HNT is for use with the POPHINT.EXE utility. SOGGY.WLK explains how to solve individual puzzles. SHADES.WLK takes you step by step through the whole adventure. But please... try to work this one out for yourself. It's worth the effort.

SOS: Son of Stagefright, The Sequel

by Mike McCauley

SOS (see Figure A-8) is the winner of the 1989 Adventure Game Toolkit contest. The object of the game is to find your way out of an old abandoned theater. Along the way you'll run into creaky catwalks, raging rivers, mini mazes, rogues, royalty, rats, and a zoo keeper. You will endure puns, perils, pratfalls, word play, bad jokes, and a mild innuendo or two.

There are 28 ways to die here. Mostly little things like falls, explosions, drowning, transmutations, liquification, broken heart, embarrassment, old age, fire, mincing, and the ever popular collapsing room. Because you're an actor here, you can also break a leg.

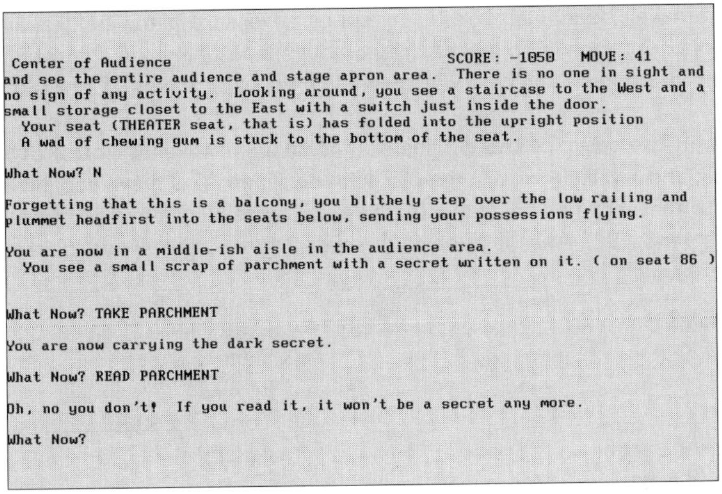

Figure A-8.
SON OF STAGEFRIGHT
Here's the quick way down.

Directory: \APPNDXA\SOS
To Play: **SOS.BAT**
Date: 1-3-94
Archive: SOS.ZIP
Registration: $5 (gets you the solution and a map)

Contact: Mike McCauley
1442 Sorrel St.
Simi Valley, CA 93065

THIEF: The Multi-Dimensional Thief

by Joel Finch

Thief (seen in Figure A-9) is the other winner of the 1991 Adventure Game Toolkit contest, sharing honors with Cosmoserve. You are trying to earn the title of master thief in this innovative adventure, and you must find your way through multiple universes, getting in and out of some very clever puzzles and traps. Fortunately, you do have

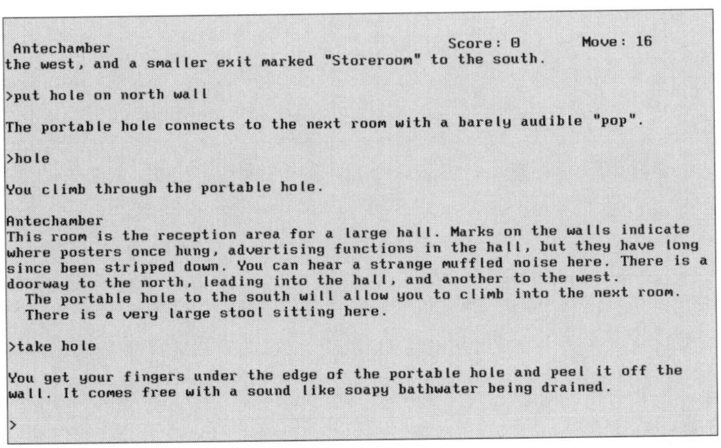

Figure A-9.
THE MULTI-DIMENSIONAL THIEF.
It's a hole new adventure!

one useful tool that has never been available in any other adventure game before or since — the portable hole. Just apply it to a wall, step through, and peel it off the other side. Talk about a feeling of power! You're going to be able to steal anything. At least, you'll think you should.

This game is written in the spirit of the original Colossal Cave; it takes you up to heaven and down to hell, and a variety of strange places in between. You may recognize a few of those places, but that may not be as much a help as you think. Remember what Steve Martin said, "Let's get small." And be sure you're wearing the right shoes, otherwise you can't go home again.

Directory:	\APPNDXA\THIEF
To Play:	**THIEF.BAT**
Date:	4-15-92
Archive:	THIEF.ZIP
Registration:	$25 prize for beating the author's record of 196 moves.

Contact: Joel Finch
Electric Sheep
Box 731
Toowong 4066
Australia

APPENDIX B

UTILITIES

SLOWDOWN UTILITIES

Many machines have a TURBO button on the front panel. Turning the Turbo mode off will usually reduce the machine's speed by half. This is useful if some of the speed-sensitive games in this collection are too fast to play.

If this doesn't work and your machine is still too fast for some of the arcade and action games, we are including several slowdown utilities. You can copy them to the game directory, or to your \DOS directory so they are accessible throughout your system.

Generally, you'll want to run one (or more) of these utilities before booting any game that runs too fast. We found that 486SLOW in combination with SLOWMO or VARISLOW was *very* effective in slowing down a 486DX2/66. You'll have to experiment to see which works best for you. Your local mileage *will* vary.

Slowgame

Directory: \APPNDXB\SLOWGAME
To Run: **SLOWGAME.COM**
Date: 6-18-91
Archive: SLOWGAME.ZIP
Registration: $10 (for source code)

Contact: Chris BoVee
Box 7821
Hollywood, FL 33081

486Slow

Directory: \APPNDXB\486SLOW
To Run: **ICE.EXE, ICD.EXE** (enable, disable)
Date: 10-5-91
Archive: 486SLOW.ZIP

Contact: Michael Spertus
CompuServe: 70313,2520

SlowDown

Directory: \APPNDXB\SLOWDOWN
To Run: **SLOWDOWN.COM**
Date: 1-30-92
Archive: SLOWDOWN.ZIP

SlowMo

Directory: \APPNDXB\SLOWMO
To Run: **SLOWMO.COM**
Date: 1-28-87
Archive: SLOWMO.ZIP

VariSlow

Directory: \APPNDXB\VARISLOW
To Run: **VARISLOW.COM**
Date: 6-24-86
Archive: VARISLOW.ZIP

ABOUT THIS BOOK

HOW WE SELECTED GAMES

Every game in this collection was play-tested at least three times before the final decision was made to include it. There is no game in this book that I did not personally check for playability. Many of the games demanded extensive play-testing. In addition, most of the games were also inspected by my nine-year-old son Dennis (a trained professional) who generously contributed his unbiased opinions.

The primary criterion for inclusion was *playability*. Quality of presentation was also a consideration, but several games with spectacular sound and graphics were eliminated because the frustration factor was too high. Overall, we went for entertainment value. We tried to select the best representatives in each category; although in a few cases, some games were selected for their appeal to special interests.

We also wanted to maintain a sense of historical accuracy. With the classic games, such as Adventure and Hack/Nethack, we included most of the major versions so that the contributions of many authors and programmers could be acknowledged. Although there are multiple versions of several more recent games (including Commander Keen and Paganitzu), ancillary factors kept us from including every implementation. And some older programs had to be left out because they were just too speed-sensitive to be playable on current machines.

Several games were eliminated because they were not true shareware, only demos of commercial programs. Some games were skipped because we had just too many in a category to choose from. A few were selected, then discarded for reasons of appropriateness. We found one excellent chess game that we could not use because there was no documentation to say if it was freeware or shareware. Another game was a bootleg version of a discontinued commercial product. Two were dropped at the request of their publishers. Two more were eliminated on the recommendations of experienced gamers.

The result of this winnowing process was an overall tightening of direction. We found ourselves focusing our efforts in three areas: classics and other games of historical interest; representative types and games of special appeal, and finally, games that represent the state of the art. In each of these areas, we worked to provide a wide selection of excellent examples, calling special attention to those we thought were truly outstanding.

But... we must also acknowledge that some games were not included because we just didn't know about them. For that we apologize. We hope to find all of the ones we missed that should have been here before we publish *Fatal Distractions 2*.

By all means, send us your best recommendations.

SOURCES OF SHAREWARE

The games in this collection were located from a number of sources. We'd like to acknowledge the best of them:

Internet: The largest network in the world is Internet. It is often confusing and difficult for newcomers, but there is a great deal of assistance available for the beginner, and Internet access will only become easier in the future. The Internet is a great source for information about specific games, such as Nethack, Wolfenstein, and Doom. Often, you will find material on the Internet that is not generally available elsewhere.

CompuServe: For sheer ease of use and volume of available material, CompuServe cannot be beaten. CIS is the largest of all on-line services. A number of forums have games stored in their libraries, but four in particular are worth noting. The GAMERS forum has many of the best shareware games in their library, and their message sections are filled with lively discussions on game design, hints, cheats, and what's coming up next. The EPIC forum is run by Epic MegaGames, and is the best source for information and new releases from Epic. The PBS (Public Brand Software) forum should also be on your list of places to explore. Public Brand Software has an extensive collection of shareware, and you can easily spend a day or two just browsing through the catalog. There is also an ASP forum for the Association of Shareware Professionals, where the concerns of shareware authors and distributors are discussed; the ASP library has many fine programs. Write to CompuServe at 5000 Arlington Centre Blvd., P.O. Box 20212, Columbus, OH 43220, or call 800-848-8990.

Public (software) Library: This is a monthly review of new shareware offerings, published by shareware author Nelson Ford. Individual programs can be ordered from PsL, or you can subscribe to the monthly CD-ROM which includes all of the new programs. The CD-ROM also includes a rotating selection of PsL's entire library, so if you subscribe for six months, you will end up with the entire catalog on disc. Write to Public (software) Library at P.O. Box 35705, Houston, TX 77235-5705, or call 800-242-4775.

Computer Swap Meets: Check your local computer publications for the times and locations of swap meets nearest you. There will invariably be shareware dealers with bins of floppy disks for you to browse through. Programs are usually distributed one per disk; pricing is generally $3 per disk. If you buy five disks, some dealers give you the sixth one free. While we cannot endorse any local shareware dealer, we have personally met many who work very hard to keep their catalogs up-to-date.

Bulletin Board Systems: There are thousands of bulletin board systems in the United States. Every major city has scores of special-interest boards. Some systems specialize in games and shareware. Again, you will have to check your local computer publications for listings of Bulletin Board Systems. Several gaming companies, including Apogee, also maintain their own BBS outlets. Check the documentation that comes with the games.

Shareware Distribution Catalogs: There are several excellent shareware distributors who send out monthly or quarterly catalogs. We have had very good luck with Reasonable Solutions, 1221 Disk Drive, Medford, OR 97501-6639; 800-876-3475. The Reasonable Solutions catalog is handsomely produced with many color screen shots. RS generally limits their selection to the best programs in each category. We've also found many fine programs in the Shareware Express catalog. Shareware Express is at 1908-D Ashland Street, Ashland, OR 97520, or you can call 800-346-2842. A third catalog of note comes from Computers International, P.O. Box 6085, Oceanside, CA 92058; 800-777-7207. Computers International also displays at various swap meets. The collection is extensive, and the catalog is well produced. Software Labs, 100 Corporate Pointe, Suite 195, Culver City, CA 90230 was also a valuable source for games; their phone number is 800-569-7900.

FUTURE EDITIONS

If you have any corrections, suggestions, or recommendations for games to be included in the next edition of Fatal Distractions, please write to:

Fatal Distractions
c/o Waite Group Press
200 Tamal Plaza, Suite 101
Corte Madera, CA 94925

We look forward to hearing from you.

INDEX

G

H

I

J

K

L

M

N

P

Q

R

S

T

U

V

W

X

Z

ENVIRONMENTAL AWARENESS

Books have a substantial influence on the destruction of the forests of the Earth. For example, it takes 17 trees to produce one ton of paper. A first printing of 30,000 copies of a typical 480-page book consumes 108,000 pounds of paper which will require 918 trees!

Waite Group Press™ is against the clear-cutting of forests and supports reforestation of the Pacific Northwest of the United States and Canada, where most of this paper comes from. As a publisher with several hundred thousand books sold each year, we feel an obligation to give back to the planet. We will therefore support and contribute a percentage of our proceeds to organizations which seek to preserve the forests of planet Earth.

WAITE GROUP PRESS™

EROTIC CONNECTIONS

LOVE AND LUST ON THE INFORMATION HIGHWAY

Billy Wildhack

Cold silicone and hot blood? Whatever you're looking for, there's a real possibility of finding it electronically. You can meet people "online" and get to know them, without surrendering your privacy. This book gives you step-by-step instructions on how to enter and use the adult-oriented bulletin board systems (BBSs).

November 1994 • 300 pages
Level: Beginning
ISBN: 1-878739-78-6
Platform: DOS
U.S. $24.95 Can. $37.95
Category: Cybersex/Telecomm
(Optional CD-ROM available)

WINDOWS ANIMATION FESTIVAL CD

Alberto Menache and Richard Sher, CEC3Space

The Windows-based CD-ROM contains more than 600 megabytes of award-winning animations: Broadcast and Commercial Animation, Scientific and Educational Animation, Industrial Animation, Computer Animation Art, Legal Animation. In addition to the CD, the accompanying book features understandable explanations of the concepts, as well as information about the technology used to create each movie.

August 1994 • 120 pages
Level: Beginning-Advanced
ISBN: 1-878739-70-0
Platform: Windows
U.S. $32.95 Can. $45.95

WALKTHROUGHS AND FLYBYS II:

MODELING THE DREAM

Phil Shatz

More than 500 megabytes of CD-ROM includes the best examples of computer-animated visuals on the planet: a dizzying ride through the insides of an arcade game, piloting an attack helicopter through an urban landscape, and bizarre androids fighting to the death. The book takes you behind the scenes to meet and share some secrets with the artists and programmers who created them.

August 1994 • 150 pages
Level: Beginning-Intermediate
ISBN: 1-878739-67-0
Platform: DOS
US. $32.95 Can. $45.95
Category: Graphics/Multimedia
Disk: 1-CD-ROM

WALKTHROUGHS AND FLYBYS CD

Phil Shatz

This book/CD package serves up awe-inspiring animated computer demos, complete with sound and music, and a behind-the-scenes look at their creation.

Available now • 150 pages
ISBN: 1-878739-40-9
U.S. $32.95 Can. $41.95
Disk: 1-CD-ROM

FALCON 3

Joel Powell and Tom Basham

Go from ground school to mastery of the skies and the thrill of flight with over 30 custom missions. A full-featured demo and two hot utilities are included on the disk.

Available now • 652 pages
ISBN: 1-878739-29-8
U.S. $34.95 Can. $48.95
Disk: 1 5.25"

This is a legal agreement between you, the end user and purchaser, and The Waite Group®, Inc., and the authors of the programs contained in the disk. By opening the sealed disk package, you are agreeing to be bound by the terms of this Agreement. If you do not agree with the terms of this Agreement, promptly return the unopened disk package and the accompanying items (including the related book and other written material) to the place you obtained them for a refund.

SOFTWARE LICENSE

1. The Waite Group, Inc. grants you the right to use one copy of the enclosed software programs (the programs) on a single computer system (whether a single CPU, part of a licensed network, or a terminal connected to a single CPU). Each concurrent user of the program must have exclusive use of the related Waite Group, Inc. written materials.

2. The program, including the copyrights in each program, is owned by the respective author and the copyright in the entire work is owned by The Waite Group, Inc. and they are therefore protected under the copyright laws of the United States and other nations, under international treaties. You may make only one copy of the disk containing the programs exclusively for backup or archival purposes, or you may transfer the programs to one hard disk drive, using the original for backup or archival purposes. You may make no other copies of the programs, and you may make no copies of all or any part of the related Waite Group, Inc. written materials.

3. You may not rent or lease the programs, but you may transfer ownership of the programs and related written materials (including any and all updates and earlier versions) if you keep no copies of either, and if you make sure the transferee agrees to the terms of this license.

4. You may not decompile, reverse engineer, disassemble, copy, create a derivative work, or otherwise use the programs except as stated in this Agreement.

GOVERNING LAW

This Agreement is governed by the laws of the State of California.

LIMITED WARRANTY

The following warranties shall be effective for 90 days from the date of purchase: (i) The Waite Group, Inc. warrants the enclosed disk to be free of defects in materials and workmanship under normal use; and (ii) The Waite Group, Inc. warrants that the programs, unless modified by the purchaser, will substantially perform the functions described in the documentation provided by The Waite Group, Inc. when operated on the designated hardware and operating system. The Waite Group, Inc. does not warrant that the programs will meet purchaser's requirements or that operation of a program will be uninterrupted or error-free. The program warranty does not cover any program that has been altered or changed in any way by anyone other than The Waite Group, Inc. The Waite Group, Inc. is not responsible for problems caused by changes in the operating characteristics of computer hardware or computer operating systems that are made after the release of the programs, nor for problems in the interaction of the programs with each other or other software.

THESE WARRANTIES ARE EXCLUSIVE AND IN LIEU OF ALL OTHER WARRANTIES OF MERCHANTABILITY OR FITNESS FOR A PARTICULAR PURPOSE OR OF ANY OTHER WARRANTY, WHETHER EXPRESS OR IMPLIED.

EXCLUSIVE REMEDY

The Waite Group, Inc. will replace any defective disk without charge if the defective disk is returned to The Waite Group, Inc. within 90 days from date of purchase.

This is purchaser's sole and exclusive remedy for any breach of warranty or claim for contract, tort, or damages.

LIMITATION OF LIABILITY

THE WAITE GROUP, INC. AND THE AUTHORS OF THE PROGRAMS SHALL NOT IN ANY CASE BE LIABLE FOR SPECIAL, INCIDENTAL, CONSEQUENTIAL, INDIRECT, OR OTHER SIMILAR DAMAGES ARISING FROM ANY BREACH OF THESE WARRANTIES EVEN IF THE WAITE GROUP, INC. OR ITS AGENT HAS BEEN ADVISED OF THE POSSIBILITY OF SUCH DAMAGES.

THE LIABILITY FOR DAMAGES OF THE WAITE GROUP, INC. AND THE AUTHORS OF THE PROGRAMS UNDER THIS AGREEMENT SHALL IN NO EVENT EXCEED THE PURCHASE PRICE PAID.

COMPLETE AGREEMENT

This Agreement constitutes the complete agreement between The Waite Group, Inc. and the authors of the programs, and you, the purchaser.

Some states do not allow the exclusion or limitation of implied warranties or liability for incidental or consequential damages, so the above exclusions or limitations may not apply to you. This limited warranty gives you specific legal rights; you may have others, which vary from state to state.